The Epistle to the Romans

An Expository Outline

Hamilton Smith

Scripture Truth Publications

THE EPISTLE TO THE ROMANS

Original manuscript dated 1935

First published 2008

ISBN: 978-0-901860-85-9 (paperback)

Copyright © 2008 Scripture Truth Publications

Published by Scripture Truth Publications
31-33 Glover Street,
Crewe, Cheshire, CW1 3LD

Scripture Truth is an imprint of Central Bible Hammond Trust, a charitable trust

Typesetting by John Rice
Printed and bound by Lightning Source

FOREWORD

I have had these and other manuscripts by the late Hamilton Smith in my possession for about twenty-five years. It was only recently that I realised that not all of them have been published. I know that some appreciate the writings of this servant of God and therefore I am also making these available.

In the manuscripts, capital letters have been used for words such as Apostle, Epistle, Cross, etc. Unless they begin a sentence I have substituted the lower case. I have also substituted the Roman numerals with the usual numbers to denote the chapters in the scripture references. A few spelling and quotation corrections were necessary. I have added some scripture references because not all today are as familiar with the Bible as Hamilton Smith's generation. Otherwise the text has not been changed.

If any soul is established, edified or encouraged the work will not have been in vain.

D. H.

Now to him that is of power to stablish you according to my gospel, and the preaching of Jesus Christ, according to the revelation of the mystery, which was kept secret since the world began, ... To God only wise, be glory through Jesus Christ for ever. Amen.
Romans 16:25-27

THE EPISTLE TO THE ROMANS

CONTENTS

DIVISION 1

THE RIGHTEOUSNESS OF GOD

Chapter 1:1 – 5:11

1.   INTRODUCTORY

CHAPTER 1:1-17

VERSE 1

The first seven verses of the epistle present the credentials of the apostle, the great theme of the epistle and the apostolic greetings to the saints at Rome. Not only was Paul the bondman of Jesus Christ in common with many others, but, by special calling, he was constituted an apostle. Therefore his service had an apostolic character as one specially sent forth to announce glad tidings.

The great theme of this epistle is the glad tidings of God concerning His Son. It is characteristic of this epistle that every truth is traced to God and viewed in connection with God. Thus in this chapter we have 'the gospel of God', the 'righteousness of God', 'the wrath of God', 'the truth of God' and 'the judgment of God'. Later we have 'the goodness of God', 'the oracles of God', the 'glory of God', 'the forbearance of God' and 'the love of God'.

That God should approach a guilty world with glad tidings shows the disposition of God towards His fallen creatures. It proves, indeed, that God is love; that He is a Saviour God who will have all men to be saved, and come unto the knowledge of the truth.

VERSE 2

The glad tidings announced by Paul are also confirmed by
Holy Scriptures. Promised by God's prophets in past days
they are now proclaimed by God's servants in this day of
grace. When proclaimed they have the authority of, and
confirm, the promise in Holy Writings. Hence in preaching the gospel, the apostle constantly appeals to the
Scriptures (See Acts 13:27, 47; 17:2, 11, etc.).

VERSES 3-4

Then very blessedly the apostle presents the great theme
of the gospel. The glad tidings of God are 'concerning His
Son'. They are not about us. There can be no glad tidings
concerning fallen man as such. Truly the glad tidings are
for men; but they are about the Son of God.

The apostle then presents a beautiful picture of the four-
fold glories of Christ. It is important to notice the order
in which these glories are presented — an order which is
rather obscured by our authorised version, in which 'Jesus
Christ our Lord' is placed second, whereas these words
should come at the end of verse four. First, then, Christ is
presented as the Son, speaking of His divine and eternal
Personality, unchanged by anything He became. Secondly,
Christ is presented in His incarnation 'come of David's
seed according to flesh'. This speaks not of His inherent
Personal glory, but of what He became as a perfect Man.
He was the Son before He came of the seed of David. He
did not become the Son by becoming incarnate. Thirdly,
having become flesh, the glory of His Person is carefully
guarded by the fact that in Manhood He is marked out
from all others as the Son of God, in divine power,
according to the Spirit of holiness, by resurrection. The
reference to resurrection is not only to His own resurrection, as the wrong insertion of the article might imply. It

is the fact of the exercise of the mighty power of resurrection whether in the case of Lazarus and others, or in that of His own resurrection, that marks Him out as a divine Person. Man's power is seen in devising complicated engines of war to put men to death, but all the wit of man has never been able to raise a man from the dead. God alone can raise from the dead. Moreover, declaration of divine power was 'according to the Spirit of holiness'. It was to meet the demands of holiness that the Lord Jesus came to suffer on the cross. But if holiness required the work of the cross, holiness equally demanded that the glory of the One who had stooped to accomplish that work should be declared by resurrection.

Fourthly, Christ is acknowledged to be Jesus Christ, *our Lord*. With great delight, those who believe God's testimony concerning Him come under His sway by owning Him their Lord and Master.

Verse 5

This then was the glorious Person that Paul came to present. Christ was gone from the world; but Paul is sent as an apostle to represent Christ. He comes 'on behalf of His Name'. In order that he might be a fitting representative, he had received from Christ 'grace and apostleship'. Not only apostleship, but the needed grace to exercise the apostleship. He did not receive his commission from man, or by any human training or ordination. Moreover, if he comes as the representative of Christ, 'on behalf of His Name', it is in order to bring man to submit to Christ, to bring them under the sway of Christ — to obey Him. Only those who believe will submit, hence it is said to be the 'obedience of faith'. This apostleship is to be exercised 'among all the nations'. Thus, if the glad tidings are concerning His Son Jesus Christ, they are for 'all the nations'.

It is no longer a question of one favoured nation — the Jews. The blessing of the gospel is for all.

VERSES 6-7

Among the nations the Romans had a leading place, and from this nation there were the called of Jesus Christ. To all such in Rome Paul sends this epistle with his greetings. He reminds them that they are the *called* of Jesus Christ; *beloved* of God; and, by the fact of their call, constituted saints.

VERSES 8-13

Not having seen the saints at Rome it was necessary that in the prelude he should speak of himself in greater detail than is usual in his epistles. Having fully presented his credentials, his thoughts pass on to those to whom he was writing, leading him to speak of his brotherly affection for all saints. There was that in his special service and apostolic position which impelled him to write to the saints at Rome; but there was also that in the saints themselves which drew out his affections towards them. The report of their faith had reached the apostle lifting up his heart in praise to God. Furthermore, he not only praises God on account of their faith, he also prays to God without ceasing on account of their need; as one has said, 'the sincerest faith was never beyond the need of help'. Those, moreover, for whom we can both praise and pray, are those we desire to see. Thus the apostle says, 'I long to see you'. The motive of his desire is that he might impart some spiritual gift, to the end that they might be established. This brings before us the great purpose of the epistle to the Romans — *the establishment of the believer in his personal relationships with God.*

His purpose in writing, and his desire to see them, was not only to fulfil his apostolic commission, or to exercise

apostolic authority, but was the outcome of brotherly
affection that longed after them, and counted upon
receiving comfort from them, as well as imparting spiritual blessing to them.

The apostle had often purposed coming to them, but had
been hindered. May we not see the grace and wisdom of
God in allowing a hindrance that has resulted in an
Epistle being written for the blessing of God's people in all
ages? Good for us to trace the hand of God in the things
that He hinders as well as in those that He allows; and
submit to His closed doors, as to pass through His open
doors.

VERSES 14-16

In the following verses the apostle speaks of his indebtedness, and readiness, to preach. Not only was the apostle
desirous to see these brethren, and impart unto them
some spiritual gift, but he felt as one who had a debt to
discharge. Very blessedly he can say, 'I am a debtor' to the
Gentiles. 'I am ready' to preach; and 'I am not ashamed'
of the gospel. 'I am a debtor' is the language of one who,
having found in the gospel that which meets his own
need, feels his indebtedness to tell the good news to others who are in need, whether among cultivated Greeks or
unintelligent Barbarians. 'I am ready', is the language of
one in right moral conditions to preach. 'I am not
ashamed', is the language of one who, realising the greatness of the gospel, is bold to proclaim it.

These things while true of the apostle in a special sense, as
being sent to the Gentiles, should be true in measure of
every believer. The joy of the gospel would make us
debtors to proclaim the glad tidings; a right moral condition of soul would make us *ready* to preach; and a sense of

13

the greatness of the gospel would keep us from being *ashamed* to tell others of the good news.

VERSES 16-17

The apostle closes the introduction to the epistle by presenting a beautiful epitome of the gospel, thus showing why he is not ashamed of the gospel.

First, he says, 'It is *the power of God unto salvation*'. God is its source. It is not man coming to God with his works, but God approaching man with salvation. We can understand God's power to judge a guilty sinner, but the marvel of the gospel is that it reveals God's power to save a sinner who deserves to be judged.

Secondly, it is God's power to save *'every one' that believes*, to the Jew first, and also to the Gentile. Man comes into the blessing of the gospel by faith, and 'to have part in it by faith was exactly to share it without adding anything whatsoever to it, and to leave it wholly the salvation of God' (J.N.Darby).

Thirdly, the reason it is God's power to save every one that believes is that *'therein is righteousness of God revealed'*. If there is no way whereby man can be saved righteously, there can be no salvation for man. It is obvious that whatever God does must be in righteousness. In the gospel God is revealed as acting righteously, and therefore with power to save. It is true that in the gospel we see the revelation of the love, and grace, and mercy of God: but of these blessed qualities the apostle does not speak in this passage, but of the righteousness of God. This is going to be the great theme of the early part of the epistle. As we have seen, his object in writing the epistle is to establish the believer; for this reason the apostle presses the righteousness of God. The sinner does not fear the love, or grace, or mercy of God; but he fears the righteousness of

God must be against him. The guilty sinner feels that if God knows all his sins, and acts rightly towards him, according to what his sins deserve, he must be punished. But if one can tell the sinner that the very quality in God that he most dreads — the righteousness of God — is the very quality that is for him, and not against him, this will indeed be good news, and go far to win the sinner and establish the believer.

Fourthly, the manner in which the righteousness of God is revealed is 'on the principle of faith' (N.Tr.). It is not revealed to sight, or because of any works that men have done. And if revealed on the principle of faith it can only be to those who have faith. The scripture testifies to this truth for the prophet Habbakuk says, 'the just shall live by faith' (Habbakuk 2:4).

2. THE TRIAL AND EXPOSURE OF MAN

CHAPTER 1:18 – 3:20

From the introductory verses we learn that the great end of the epistle is to establish believers in their personal relationships with God; as the apostle says, 'To the end ye may be established'. To accomplish this end the apostle shows that the gospel is God's power to save because therein is revealed the righteousness of God. Nothing will so establish the believer as the discovery that God not only saves the sinner that believes in Jesus, but that He does so righteously — that is, in consistency with His own holy nature.

Before, however, the apostle can proceed to show how God can righteously justify the sinner that believes in Jesus, it is necessary to set forth man's need of this righteousness, by showing that man has no righteousness of his own. He does this by proving that man has ruined himself, and can do nothing to save himself from his ruined condition. If, therefore, anyone is to be saved, it must entirely depend upon what God does for man, and not upon what man does for God. What God does must be in righteousness: hence the salvation of man entirely depends upon God acting righteously towards man.

The great object, therefore, of this important section of the epistle is to prove that man has no righteousness of God. To prove this the apostle goes over the history of man, and shows that man has been tested under every conceivable condition with the result that, under every test, man has completely broken down. When put into a position of responsibility, man has entirely failed to carry out his responsibilities. He has not acted rightly towards God or his neighbour. He has proved himself to be ungodly and unrighteous.

Verse 18

Verse 18 contains a general statement which covers the whole section. It is the indictment against all men, which will be fully proved by the details that follow in verses 19 to 3:20. Men are proved to be impious (N.Tr.) and unrighteous. Impiety is the contempt with which men treat the witness that God has given of Himself. Unrighteousness refers to their evil practices. Moreover, it is proved that men hold the truth in unrighteousness. The heathen, the moralist, and the Jew, all had some measure of truth, but they used the truth they had for evil purposes. The heathen turned the light of creation into an occasion for idolatry. The Jews used the law to boast in themselves. Alas! The same principle is at work in Christendom. The love of God is used to deny the holiness of God. The truth is advanced to maintain error.

Against all this evil, disclosed by the testing of man, the wrath of God is revealed. The cross that demonstrates the righteousness of God to save the sinner that believes, also demonstrates the wrath of God against sin. It is the wrath of God revealed from heaven, and it is against *all* impiety and unrighteousness. In Old Testament days God's wrath was revealed in governmental judgements that overtook certain individuals, or nations, because of certain sins committed against the partial light that they had. Now it is no longer a limited expression of wrath, according to what man is on earth, but wrath revealed according to the holy nature of God in heaven; and it is against all sin, wherever that sin may be found.

If, in the gospel, we have the full setting forth of the righteousness of God that can save, we have, at the same time, the revelation of the wrath of God against sin. God's righteousness in saving does not in the slightest degree set aside God's wrath against sin. On the contrary, the revelation of the power of God that can righteously save the greatest sinner becomes the occasion of fully declaring the wrath of God against all sin. On our side we can afford to face the full revelation of the wrath of God against sins, if we know there is righteousness with God to forgive sins. The wrath is not yet executed, for God is acting in grace, but it is revealed.

After this general indictment, the apostle proceeds to prove its truth by separately reviewing, first, the history of the heathen (1:19-32); secondly the ways of the moralist (2:1-16); thirdly the history of the Jew (2:17 – 3:18). Finally, this section of the epistle is closed with a solemn summary of man's condition, proving the whole world to be under sin and exposed to the judgement of God (3:19-20).

THE HEATHEN (1:19-32)

Passing from the general indictment of man to the details of his history, the apostle first takes up the heathen who were without a direct revelation from God. Nevertheless, they were not left without a witness from God. Their responsibility was of a threefold character:–

1   They had creation which bore witness to God (verses 19-20);

2   They had a certain knowledge of God (verses 21-31);

3   They had conscience that told them they were not acting according to their knowledge of God (verse 32).

VERSES 19-20

The witness of creation. 'From the world's creation the invisible things of him are perceived, being apprehended by the mind through the things that are made, both his eternal power and divinity, so as to render them inexcusable' (N.Tr.). Having the full light of revelation, which throws into the shade every other testimony, we are in danger of forgetting how great is the witness to God in creation. Men, alas, show their impiety by pouring contempt on every witness to God. The evolutionist seeks to explain creation by what he considers natural laws and thus would eliminate from creation all witness to God. The modernist would rob us of all knowledge of God, by leaving us without a revelation from God.

In spite of the infidelity of man's heart, whether it betrays itself in evolution or modernism, the creation remains, and the Psalmist declares, 'The heavens declare the glory of God, and the firmament sheweth his handiwork'. While creation in all its parts declares the eternal power and divinity of God, it is not a little significant, that, the inspired writer of Psalm 19 speaks of parts of the creation which man has no power to touch or corrupt. He speaks of the unceasing procession of day and night, and of the perpetual circuit of the sun. In God's estimate, so powerful and convincing is this witness to His power and divinity that it leaves man without excuse.

There is no suggestion that the creation bore witness to the gospel, or that it revealed God according to His nature; but it witnessed to the Creator, and man, instead of turning to the Creator through this witness, turned from the Creator. Men clearly showed then, as the infidel scientist shows now, that God is not wanted. Clearly, if man does not want God, he will not want God's gospel. The rejection of the witness of creation leaves man without excuse, even though he has not heard the gospel.

VERSES 21-23

The light of the knowledge of God. Beside the witness of creation, from the beginning of history men had a certain knowledge of God. To this the apostle refers when he says, 'they knew God'. The world before the flood began with a knowledge of God, and to that world Enoch prophesied and Noah preached, so that it was not left without a testimony from God. As, however, the apostle refers to idolatry, it is probable that he has mainly in view the present world which has sprung from Noah and his family. The first act of this present world was to build an altar unto the Lord, clearly showing that this present world commenced with some knowledge of God. They had just learnt by the solemn judgement of the flood that God was not indifferent to man's ways, and would not go on indefinitely with violence and corruption. Thus they knew they had to do with a God to whom man was responsible.

This knowledge of God should have led men to glorify God for all his power and wisdom in creation, and to thank Him for all His rich provision for man's blessing. Fallen man, however, whether in that day or this, fears and hates God. Men may indeed be compelled to admit the existence of some great First Cause, for they know that all their fine theories will never explain the ultimate origin of creation. But, in their insane desire to forget God, they endeavour, as one has said, to hide God behind His works, rather than discover God in them.

Neither glorifying God in His works, nor thanking God for His temporal mercies, they lost the knowledge of God that they possessed. Refusing the witness of creation, they fell back, as men are doing today, upon their own imaginations. Thus their foolish heart was darkened, that is, they lost the knowledge of God. Moral darkness is always, in Scripture, ignorance of God; even as light is the knowledge of God. The more foolish they became the more they professed to be wise: and the more they professed to be wise, the bigger fools they became.

However, man is not sufficient for himself. He must have someone upon whom to lean, someone to whom he can look in his misery and weakness. So having rejected the true God and become a fool, he proceeds to fashion false gods according to his own tastes. As men's tastes differ, so men invented a number of gods to suit their different tastes. First they conceived of God as like to corruptible men; then sinking lower in their conceptions of God, they imagined God to be like birds or four-footed beasts, until they reached the lowest depth of degradation, when they conceived of God as like the creeping things — the serpents. Thus the worship of the serpent proved how thoroughly man had fallen from God to the devil.

Verses 24-27

The appalling result is brought before us in the verses that follow. Man had given up God, now we have the statement, thrice repeated, 'that God gave them up'. In the government of God men are allowed to reap what they sow. Their lusts have turned them away from the true God; now, the false gods, they had set up according to

21

their own tastes, sanctioned and encouraged their lusts. God giving them up to their lusts, they immediately proceed to dishonour their own bodies, even as they had already dishonoured God.

Having changed the truth of God into a lie, and in place of the Creator set up the creature as an object of worship, they are permitted to fall beneath the creatures that they worshipped. Men sank below the beasts. It has been truly said a beast is not a moral creature, but a man degraded to the level of a beast becomes *immoral*. His affections become corrupted and perverted from their natural course into that which is contrary to nature.

Verses 28-31

The condition described in the verses that follow, present an awful picture of the abominations of the heathen world. The condition described by this catalogue of crimes is traced back to one root. When men had some knowledge of God, 'They did not think good to have God in their knowledge' (N.Tr.). Men deliberately gave up the light that God had given of Himself, with the result that man is given over to a reprobate mind, abandoned to his depraved thoughts. Thus the awful effect of sin is to leave men with defiled *bodies* (verse 24), degraded *affections* (verse 26) and depraved *minds*. Man is fallen, body, soul and spirit. Scripture also makes abundantly clear that the condition of the last stage of Christendom will be such that it can only be described in terms almost similar to this list of vices. In 2 Timothy 3:1-5, the apostle shows that the condition of Christendom will sink to the condition of heathendom; and the same root will produce the same fruit, for in 2 Timothy 4:4 the apostle, speaking of professing Christians in these last difficult days, says, 'they shall turn away their ears from the truth, and shall be turned unto fables'.

In the early days of the world's history men had a measure of knowledge of God that left them without excuse. They deliberately gave up this knowledge of God. 'They did not think good to have God in their knowledge', and they sunk below the beasts.

In these days, we have the full knowledge of God, who once dwelt in thick darkness, but has now come into the light. In the Person of the Son, God has been fully revealed. Again we find that men are turning away their ears from the truth, and turning unto fables. Christendom, like the men of old, does not think it good to have God in their knowledge. There is, however, this solemn difference, in the former day men turned away from a partial knowledge of God; today men are turning from the full knowledge of God in Christianity. The result will be all the more appalling. Our only safety is to see that we retain the knowledge of God according to the light in which He has revealed Himself in Christ.

VERSE 32

The witness of conscience. Finally we learn that from the beginning man had the witness of conscience within him. He knows that the sins that he loves and commits are wrong and entail punishment. He refuses the witness of creation; he does not see good to retain the knowledge of God; so too, he neglects the voice of conscience.

Thus the heathen world is proved to be a ruined world, without any excuse for its evil, and without righteousness for God.

THE MORALIST (2:1-16)

VERSE 1

The apostle has presented a vivid picture of the awful degradation of heathendom. In spite, however, of its fearful corruption, man retains the ability to judge, and condemn, the evil in his fellow men. This ability, in itself, is a proof that we are fallen creatures: for the knowledge of good and evil was only acquired by the fall. In the midst of heathendom there arose a class of men called philosophers, who, by the cultivation of their intellectual powers, developed this ability to judge of evil, to a very high degree.

In the first portion of the second chapter (verses 1-16), the apostle exposes these philosophic moralists, wherever they may be found, whether among the heathen, the Jews or in Christendom. Already he has shown that the witness of creation leaves men without excuse; now he will show that the ability to condemn evil also leaves men without excuse; for the plain reason that the ability to condemn evil gives no power to resist evil. Thus while condemning evil men commit the very evils they condemn.

The question therefore arises, will the fact that man has the ability to condemn evil, enable man to escape the righteous judgement of God, if the man commits the evil that he condemns? There can be only one answer to this question — such will not escape the judgement of God.

This leads the apostle to unfold four deeply important principles of God in regard to His judgement of evil and evil-doers: each of these principles utterly condemning the moralist and leaving him exposed to the judgement of God.

24

VERSES 2-3

The first great principle of God's judgement of evil is, *'that the judgement of God is according to truth'*. The standard by which God measures evil is not the standard of philosophy, but the 'truth' as to God made known in Christianity. All that God is has been made known in Christ. 'Grace and *truth* came by Jesus Christ'. Now that the full truth of all that God is, in His holy nature, has been revealed, it becomes the standard by which God judges all evil. Men measure evil by standards that they set up. Philosophers measure evil by their own systems of philosophy; the Mohammedans by the Koran, and other false systems by their sacred books. God's judgement of evil is according to the truth of all that He is in His own holy nature as revealed in Christ.

Verse 2 presents the *moral judgement* of God in regard to evil. Verse 3 and the following verses look on to the *execution of judgement* in the day of judgement. If God passes judgement according to the truth of His holy nature, it is very certain that those who practice what they condemn in others will not escape the execution of the judgement of God, unless they repent.

VERSES 4-5

This leads to the assertion of the second great principle of God in regard to judgement, namely, *God invariably gives space for repentance before He executes judgement.* The execution of the judgement of God will most surely come, though it may be long delayed. In His goodness God forbears to judge and suffers long with evil. It was so in the days of Noah, when God lingered for one hundred and twenty years before executing the judgement of the flood: it was so in the history of Israel, with whose evil ways God bore long before destroying Jerusalem and scattering the nation. It is so today when God in grace lingers over this judgement doomed world. How then does man treat this longsuffering of God? Alas, men despise the riches of His goodness. Because of this 'forbearance' men think that God will never judge: because of His 'longsuffering' men think that God is indifferent to evil. Thus men despise the goodness of God, not seeing that the reason God 'forbears' and 'suffers long' is to give men space for repentance. The goodness of God thus makes manifest the hardness and impenitence of man's heart. God acts in goodness, and men despise 'the riches of His goodness'. God gives space to repent, and men are impenitent. Men condemn one another for doing evil, but they refuse to repent of their own evil. The fact that God gives space for repentance shows that repentance is a necessity for each man in order to be right with God, and escape the judgement of God.

Paul sums up his gospel by saying he preached 'Repentance toward God, and faith toward our Lord Jesus Christ' (Acts 20:21). Repentance is the confession toward God of our lost and ruined condition. Faith is the acceptance of the good news concerning Christ. One has said, 'Repentance and faith are inseparable where there is reality; … as there is no genuine repentance without faith, so there is no faith of God's elect without repentance' (W.Kelly). Repentance is more than sorrow for having done wrong, or the shame that mere natural conscience may feel. Repentance is the change of mind in regard to self, produced by the knowledge of the grace of God. It is the consciousness and confession of my true condition before God. Repentance toward God is the acceptance of what God says about myself. Faith towards our Lord Jesus Christ is the acceptance of what God says about Christ. Peter repented when he said, in the presence of the Lord,

'I am a sinful man'. The publican repented when he said, 'God be merciful to me the sinner': the prodigal repented when he said in the presence of the father, 'I have sinned against heaven, and in thy sight': the thief repented when he said, 'We receive the due reward of our deeds'. There may be different measures of repentance, even as there are different measures of faith. With some repentance may be deeper, and faith more distinct and simple than in others; but, wherever there is a work of God in the soul, there these two things will be found.

Nor are repentance and faith to be viewed as things done once for all. Repentance deepens the more we have to do with God, and faith continually goes out toward our Lord Jesus Christ. It has been truly said of repentance that it 'will in one sense, deepen all one's life, as the knowledge of God grows'; and of faith, the same servant of God said 'Although faith in the work of Christ is necessary in order to possess peace, yet His Person ever remains as the object of the heart — the Christ Who has loved us, Who is now glorified at the right hand of God, after having borne our sins, and submitted to death and the curse for us, but ever living for us now' (J.N.Darby).

Refusing to repent, man treasures up wrath against the day of wrath. Not only does man call down wrath by his evil, but also because he despises the goodness of God that would meet the evil. All this will become manifest to the unrepentant in the day of wrath. In the goodness of God that day may be long delayed, nonetheless, it is surely coming — an actual day when *God's judgement*, not man's will be revealed and executed.

VERSES 6-10

The third great principle of God's judgement is, that *in judgement God 'will render to every man according to his deeds'*. It is not here stated when God will do this as regards 'well doing'; but in regard to evil doing it is clearly stated to be in the 'day of wrath'. Nor does the apostle say that God will judge every man, for only the evil doer comes into judgement in the 'day of wrath'. But God will *'render'* to every man according to his deeds.

On the one hand there are those, who in patient continuance of good works, seek for glory, honour and incorruptibility. To such God will render eternal life. On the other hand, there are those who are contentious and do not obey the truth of Christianity, but obey unrighteousness, whose works are evil. Such will come under the indignation and wrath of God; and not only this, they will also suffer 'tribulation and anguish'. 'Indignation and wrath' describe God's attitude towards evil doers; 'tribulation and anguish' describe their portion. In contrast to these, the portion of those who work good will be 'glory, honour and peace', even as the attitude of God toward such will be displayed in the sphere of 'eternal life'.

In these verses it is not a question of how a man enters the path of 'well doing', or by what power he continues in that path, but that which God takes account of is reality of walk, and not mere profession or privileges, such as the Jew or an enlightened philosopher might boast in. We may note also, in regard to the well doer, God does not say, 'to them who obey the truth', as this might be thought to leave out the walk. Then, too, in regard to the evil doer, God does not simply say 'unto them that obey unrighteousness', as this would leave out the truth. It must be remembered that in judgement God will not only deal with men for their evil deeds, but also for the way they have despised the truth.

Further it should be noticed that in executing judgement, or bestowing blessing, God maintains the leading place that He has given the Jew among the nations, and therefore, whether in judgement or blessing, it is 'the Jew first and also the Gentile'.

VERSES 11-16

This leads to the fourth great principle of God's judgement, that in judgement *'There is no respect of persons with God'*.

While God maintains the place He has given the Jew, yet God is no respecter of persons, and therefore the Jew will not escape because he is a privileged Jew, nor will the Gentile be able to plead he is only a poor ignorant Gentile.

VERSE 12

The fact of not having the law will be no excuse for the Gentile who has sinned without it: and the fact of having the law will not shelter the Jew who has sinned under it. Those who have sinned without it will perish without it: those who have sinned under it will be judged by it. This brings out the important principle that, in rendering to every man his deeds, God takes into account the measure of light a man has had. We have already seen that when it is a question of the sin, God measures it according to the truth of what He is; but when it is a question of measuring out retribution to the sinner, God takes into account the privileges he may have had under the law, or otherwise. This will become manifest in the day when God shall judge the secrets of men.

VERSES 13-15

Verses 13 to 15 form a parenthesis showing, firstly, it would be useless for Jewish moralists to plead they have heard the law; the question is, are they doers of the law? 'Hearing' would not justify, but 'doing'; and none have kept the law. Secondly, it would be useless for the Gentile moralists to plead they have not the law, for, as a matter of fact, the Gentile requires no law to tell him not to murder, nor steal, nor bear false witness. His own nature tells him these things are wrong, and therefore he is a law unto himself. The fact that we know these things to be wrong shows clearly that the 'works' that the law requires are written in our hearts. This is the knowledge of good and evil acquired at the fall and that all men possess. This knowledge may vary, but all men possess some measure of light as to good and evil.

Furthermore, not only have all men a measure of light, they have also a conscience which bears witness according to the measure of light possessed. Conscience is not the light, and therefore is no guide. The compass will not guide the ship; only the rudder will guide under the control of the helmsman. But the compass will tell the helmsman directly he is off the course; so conscience will bear witness directly we cease to walk according to the light we have. Then the mind acts either by listening to, or stifling, conscience — accusing or excusing.

Thus we have disclosed to us the four great principles of God's ways in judgement. God judges morally of men's evil by the standard of truth; God gives space for repentance before executing judgement: in the execution of judgement, God will render to every man according to his deeds; finally, in judgement God will be no respecter of persons.

Those who despise the goodness of God and refuse to repent will at last find themselves judged according to these principles in the day that God has fixed for the judgement — a judgement that will be carried out by Jesus Christ, Who has been appointed to judge the secrets of men. This has been revealed as the dark background of the gospel. The grace of God is presented to man in the gospel; if men refuse the grace of God they are warned that they will have to meet the judgement of God, executed by the very One — Jesus Christ — through Whom the grace is presented.

THE RELIGIOUS MAN (2:17 – 3:8)

Beginning with verse 17 of chapter 2, the apostle takes up the case of the Jew — or religious man. He has proved that the heathen, and the philosopher, are without righteousness and under judgement before God; but what of the Jew with all his religious advantages? Is he, too, under judgement; and does he require a Saviour?

To answer these questions the apostle will give a detailed description of the religious man and his advantages (verses 17-20). Then he will show how entirely the Jew has failed in carrying out the responsibilities that such advantages entail (verses 21-29).

VERSES 17-20

To show the responsibilities of the religious Jew, the apostle gives a detailed description of the advantages which pertain to the Jew, and in which he boasts. The Jew takes his stand upon the fact that he is a privileged Jew, apart from the Gentiles: next, he rests on the fact that he has a divinely given law: then, he boasts that he has the knowledge of the true God; moreover, he boasts in knowing the will of God, and that he is able to approve the things that are excellent being instructed out of the law. Being a Jew, and having the law he assumes to guide the blind, to give light to those in darkness, to instruct the foolish and teach the ignorant. Moreover, he has the form of knowledge,

31

THE EPISTLE TO THE ROMANS

and of the truth, embodied in the law. He is not dependent for the light that he has, upon mere tradition handed down from mouth to mouth.

We have only to read these verses to see how exactly they describe the religious man, whether Jew or professing Christian. Change the name Jew to Christian, and law to Bible, and we have an exact description of the Christian profession. The professing Christian boasts that he is called a Christian, and is not a heathen; that he has the Bible and the knowledge of the true God; that he is instructed by the Bible as to what is right, and is therefore able to send out missionaries to instruct the heathen.

Will, however, any, or all, of these undoubted advantages, secure the salvation of his soul, or give him a standing before God in righteousness? Will it avail before God that a man is *called* a Christian, and possesses the Bible, and is therefore able to approve what is right?

VERSES 21-23

To answer these questions, the apostle, in the verses that follow, tests the pretensions of the religious man by asking some searching questions:–

1   Addressing the religious man, the apostle asks, as it were — What about *yourself?* You have been boasting of teaching others, teachest thou thyself?

2   What about your *practice?* You preach to others that they should not steal. Dost thou steal?

3   What about the *world?* You profess to approve the things that are more excellent: Do you form unholy alliances with the world? Dost thou commit adultery?

4   What about the *heathen?* You profess to abhor idols
       — dost thou commit sacrilege?

5   What about the *law* and the *Bible?* You boast in the
       law, do you obey it?

6   What about *God?* You boast in the knowledge of
       God — Do you honour God?

These searching questions thoroughly expose the religious
man. His practice belies his profession. He has indeed the
form of godliness, but without the power. His profession
is far above the heathen, but his practice is no better.

VERSE 24

The result is summed up in one solemn statement. The
name of God is blasphemed among the Gentiles through
the religious man. The apostle is speaking of the Jew; but
what he says is equally true of the professing Christian.
The blasphemies of infidels have been mainly called forth
by the corruptions, and the degraded practices of professing Christendom. Men would not indeed have turned
Christians simply because Christians were consistent in
practice; but if Christians were in their practice true to
their profession, men would have no occasion to blas-
pheme God.

VERSES 25-29

The apostle has shown that the practice of the religious
man is far below his profession. In the verses that follow
he shows the reason for this breakdown. The root of the
failure lies in the *profession of outward privileges without an
inward work of grace in the heart.* The outward place of
privilege, of which circumcision is the sign, is indeed of
profit, if the law is kept. An outward place among the
people of God has its advantages; but if the practice is not
in accord with the place, it has no *spiritual value.* If the

33

Gentile, without the position, keeps the righteousness of the law, he would get the blessing of the privileged class, though not having their position. Therefore what is inward is of far greater importance than what is outward. The true Jew is one in whom there is an inward work of the heart, and who serves God in spirit and not in the letter, and who lives before God, and not merely before men.

The apostle has thus proved the religious professor to be, like the heathen and the moralist, without righteousness and under judgement before God. The arguments, however, that he has used in reference to the religious man, may raise three questions which he takes up and answers in the first eight verses of chapter 3.

CHAPTER 3 VERSES 1-2

First, the question may be raised: Is there no advantage in an outward position? This question arises from the fact that the apostle has just shown that the position of the religious man, with all its advantages, if not accompanied by an inward work in the heart, will give no standing *before God*. Thus the question arises: What advantage is there in outward religious privileges, such as the Jew enjoyed? Or, what profit is there in circumcision — the rite that introduced into this outward position?

In his reply the apostle definitely asserts that there are advantages in an outward position. He says, indeed, there is 'much every way'. The chief advantage being that the Jew had the oracles of God. To have the Scriptures was then, as it is now, a great gain. Even if some do not accept the gospel, it is an immense advantage to be in a land where the light of God's word is brought to bear upon men, even if it only affects their outward lives.

VERSES 3-4

The apostle's reply to the first question raises a second question. He has stated that it is a distinct advantage to have the oracles of God; but, What if some do not believe? Will their unbelief make the word of God any the less effectual for those who have 'the faith of God'? Or will the unbelief of man affect the truth of what God has said?

In reply to this question the apostle says, 'Far be the thought'. He then quotes from Psalm 51 to show that, whatever men may believe or do, God will be justified in all His sayings. In this penitential Psalm, David owns that in the judgement that overtook him, because of his great sin, God proved that all that He had said as to judgement overtaking the sinner, was true. God justified His own words in His dealings with David.

This is a solemn warning for all, believers and unbelievers alike. If we will not learn in God's presence that what God says is true, as to the evil of our hearts and the effect of sinning, we shall have to learn by coming under govern-mental judgement, or eternal judgement (in the case of unbelievers).

These chapters bring before us the solemn truth as to our-selves. Good for us if, as believers, we allow the Word to search us personally and thus learn that what God says about us is true, rather than have to learn the truth by some terrible fall as in the case of David. In one way or another we have to learn that what God says about the flesh is true, and everything that man may say to the con-trary is a lie, whoever the man may be. However great a genius, or philosopher, let him be a liar, if he contradicts what God has said as to sin and the flesh.

VERSES 5-8

We have seen that David's unrighteousness became the occasion of showing that God was right in all that He had said. Thus our unrighteousness commends God's righteousness. This raises, in the natural mind, a third question. How can God inflict judgement for doing something which though wrong, turned to the glory of God?

In speaking thus the apostle is careful to say that he is only voicing the thoughts of man. For himself he knows the argument is false, for at once he replies, 'Far be the thought'. Such an argument, if true, would make it impossible for God to judge the world.

If, says man, the truth of God has become more manifestly true through my denial of it, then my denial has become the occasion of bringing glory to God; and, in this case, why am I judged as a sinner, instead of being praised for doing evil that good may come? This apparently was what man slanderously said was the outcome of the Christian teaching, that where sin abounded grace did much more abound.

Paul has a short answer for those who argue in this fashion. He simply says, their judgement is just. Thus it becomes plain that the fact of man's sin turning to the glory of God, will not relieve man from his responsibility, or save him from the judgement of God.

ALL THE WORLD GUILTY (3:9-20)

The apostle has proved that the heathen, the moralist, and the religious man, are without any righteousness for God. He now sums up this section of the epistle, which proves the complete ruin of man, by quoting Scriptures which clearly show that all the world is guilty before God.

He has just argued that the place of outward privilege is a distinct advantage to the religious man. Are we then to understand that the Jew is morally better than the Gentile? The apostle asks: Are we Jews better than the Gentiles? In reply the apostle at once asserts that he has already proved that both Jew and Gentile are 'All under sin'. He then proceeds to show the complete ruin of all men, by quoting seven passages from the Old Testament Scriptures, which give a solemn description of man after the flesh. These Scriptures apply to both Jew and Gentile, proving that all are under sin, and that the Jew is no better than the Gentile.

The first quotation is from Psalm 14. In this Psalm the quotation is connected with the statement that 'Jehovah looked down from heaven upon the children of men, to see if there were any that did understand, and seek God'. The statements that follow, give the result of God's searching gaze. The truth presented is not, therefore, a description of how we appear before one another, but how we appear before God, as fallen children of Adam — as in the flesh. In the quotations from this Psalm, God strips us of everything in which we might boast, as natural men — the things by which we naturally seek to justify ourselves before God.

First God strips us of our self righteousness. It is written, 'There is none righteous, no, not one'. It is hard for us to believe that all our righteousnesses are as filthy rags, and that there is not one righteous in God's sight. We might plead surely there are a few; but God says, 'Not one'. This does not imply that there are no honest men amongst men; but that *not one of us has given God His rights*. It would only be right that we should love God with all our heart, with all our soul, and with all our mind; but no-one has done so, therefore no-one is righteous before God.

Secondly, 'There is none that understandeth'. The intelligence of man is very great, but with all his knowledge he does not understand God. It is notorious that the most intellectual men are generally the most ignorant of God. It was the intellectual princes of this world who crucified the Lord of glory (1 Corinthians 2:8). The truth is that neither natural wisdom, nor reason, will ever give us any true knowledge of God, or of our own hearts.

Thirdly, 'There is none that seeketh after God'. The religion of the natural man has the appearance of seeking after God. Nevertheless a religion of works, barren moralities, and ritual observances, so far from seeking God, is, in reality an effort to quiet conscience, and keep God at a distance. Fallen man may be intensely religious, but does not really seek after God.

Fourthly, 'They are all gone out of the way'. This describes the self-will of the flesh that deliberately forsakes God's way, and chooses its own way. It is not simply that we are out of the way, but that the natural man deliberately turns his back on God and takes a way of his own choosing. The prodigal deliberately left his father's house and went his own way.

Fifthly, 'They are *together* become unprofitable'. Not only does the flesh choose its own path, but men drag one another down. Men seek to forget God in the social circle. If the self-will of the prodigal led him to choose his own way and so travel into the far country — having arrived there — he plunged into the social round and sought to forget his father in company with a crowd of evil-doers.

Sixthly, 'There is none that doeth good, no, not one'. Man may do a great many philanthropic deeds, for the benefit of his fellow man; but self, or man, is the motive, not God. If the motive is not good, nothing will make the act good in the sight of God.

Thus the word of God strips the flesh of every covering by which man seeks to hide his true condition from himself, from his fellow men, and from God. Self-righteousness, intellectual efforts, religious flesh, the will of the flesh, social efforts and benefactions, are but fig leaf coverings by which men seek to hide their nakedness and pretend to be, before one another, what they are not.

Having stripped off these fig leaves, fallen man stands revealed in his true character as seen by God. In the Scriptures that follow, the throat, the tongue, the lips, the mouth and the feet, are used to set forth the different evil qualities of the flesh.

The second Scripture quoted is from Psalm 5:9, where we read, 'Their throat is an open sepulchre; they flatter with their tongue'. The throat discloses the utter corruption of the flesh — it is an open sepulchre. This corruption shows itself by lying lips.

The third quotation is from Psalm 140:3 — 'Adders' poison is under their lips'. The corruption of the flesh leads to lying; and lying leads to the poison of slander; for the flesh that can lie to your face will slander you behind your back.

The fourth quotation is from Psalm 10:7 — 'His mouth is full of cursing'. Lying leads to slander, and slander leads to cursing; for the man that is slandered will retaliate with cursing and bitterness.

The fifth quotation is from Proverbs 1:16 — 'Their feet run to evil, and they make haste to shed blood'. From 'cursing and bitterness' it is but a short way to murder.

The sixth quotation is from Isaiah 59:7-8 — 'Wasting and destruction are in their paths; the way of peace they know not'. Murder leaves in its wake ruin and misery.

The seventh quotation is from Psalm 36:1 — 'There is no fear of God before his eyes'. Ruin and misery rob men of peace. When peace is gone, men may indeed fear one another, but there is no fear of God before their eyes.

Thus the fallen man, having been first stripped of every covering, stands revealed as corrupt, lying, slandering, cursing and murdering; leaving ruin and misery in his wake; and treading a path in which there is no peace, and no fear of God. Such is the solemn picture of fallen man under the eye of God. It is not that every one of these traits will be seen in each individual, for there are many restraints upon the manifestation of the flesh in its full evil. In the ordinary walks of life there are the restraints of education, civilisation, and the outward forms of religion, which hinder the flesh showing itself in all its full wickedness. However, given the suited circumstances, the flesh will break through all restraints, and manifest itself in all its hideousness.

The cross, which is the greatest expression of the love of God, became the greatest occasion for man to express the evil of his heart. There we see the utter corruption of the flesh: Pilate can speak of Christ as a 'just person'; own that he can 'find no fault in Him'; admit that He has done 'nothing worthy of death', and yet deliberately deliver Him up to be crucified. Could there be a greater expression of the corruption of the flesh?

Then mark the lying tongue. The corruption of the flesh in Judas expresses itself in the tongue that uses deceit. He acted as well as uttered a lie, when, at the betrayal, he said: 'Hail Master', and kissed Him. Then we see the poison of the asps in the Jew; for with false witnesses and false words they slander the Lord and seek to poison the mind of Pilate against the Lord. They said, 'We found this fellow perverting the nation and forbidding to give tribute to Cæsar'. From slander they pass to cursing and bitterness, for we read, 'The chief priests stood and vehemently accused Him'. And it is but a short journey they take from anger to murder, for they said, 'Let Him be crucified'. Ruin and misery followed in the wake of this, the most terrible of all murders, even as the Lord's own words foretold, when He said, 'Behold the days are coming in the which they shall say, Blessed are the barren, and the wombs that never bare and the paps that never gave suck. Then shall they begin to say to the mountains fall on us; and to the hills cover us' (Luke 23:29-30).

Moreover the murder that brought ruin, robbed man of peace, for at the cross we read, 'All the people that came together to that sight, beholding the things which were done, smote their breasts' (Luke 23:48). There was no peace in those breasts. All this, too, was done without any fear of God, for all the people said, 'His blood be on us and on our children'.

Such then is the solemn truth as to fallen man. His ruin, and utter wickedness, as recorded in the Scripture, and demonstrated at the cross, is shown to be complete. Good for us if we justify God in His Words, not only admitting that what God has said is true about men generally, but that it is the truth as to each one of us individually — that, however much the flesh may have been restrained by particular circumstances, yet this is its true character.

This then is the testimony of the law, from which neither Jew or Gentile can escape. The Jew, who holds an outwardly advantageous position, by having the law, is utterly condemned by the law, for it is obvious that the law speaks to those who are under the law. The Jew, therefore, has no moral superiority over the Gentile. The solemn conclusion of the whole indictment is that Jew and Gentile are brought on to one common level before God. Every mouth is stopped, and all the world is under judgement before God.

VERSE 20

Moreover the law, that brings all under judgement to God, holds out no possibility of man removing the judgement by any efforts of his own. 'By the deeds of the law shall no flesh be justified in His sight'. The law, indeed, convicts of sin, 'for by the law is the knowledge of sin', but it cannot remove the sins, or deliver from the power of sin. The law is but a plumb line to show the crookedness of the wall. It would be as foolish to think that a crooked wall could be made straight by holding a plumb line against it, as to think that a guilty sinner could be justified by the law. Thus the law convicts us of not only being sinners before God, but also of being helpless sinners. Our ruin is total, and irretrievable, as far as we are concerned. Man is not only a fallen creature driven out from paradise, he cannot find his way back. The law which was given for life, if a man kept it, has become a ministration of death and condemnation.

3. THE RIGHTEOUSNESS OF GOD IN FORGIVING

CHAPTER 3:21-31

In the previous section of the epistle (1:18 – 3:20) the apostle has revealed the condition of the world before God. The result being, as proved by Scripture, every mouth is stopped and all the world is under judgement to God. Plainly, then, all is over with man, so far as man, himself, is concerned. If anyone is to be saved from judgement all must depend upon God. Therefore, at this point in the epistle, we pass from the contemplation of what man is before God, to learn what God is for guilty man. It is no longer man in his ruin, but, God in His glory that is before our souls.

VERSE 21

If, however, God acts for man it must be in righteousness. Thus at this point the apostle resumes the great subject of 'the righteousness of God', already referred to in the introduction (1:17). The righteousness of God is that quality in God which ever leads God to act according to His rights or, in other words, act in perfect consistency with Himself in relation to others.

It is natural for a convicted sinner to dread the righteousness of God. He argues that if a holy God deals rightly with a guilty sinner, it can only be to judge him for his sins. It never occurs to the sinner that God can righteously forgive his sins. When, however, we are instructed in the righteousness of God, we discover that the very quality in God that we deem to be against us, is the very quality that, above all others, is for us as sinners; and is the solid foundation of our peace as believers.

This righteousness of God is manifest in the gospel, altogether apart from the law. The law demanded righteousness from man that he was unable to render. The gospel declares God's righteousness to man, without making any demand upon man. The law *witnessed* to the righteousness of God. The sacrifices under the law, and the utterances of the prophets, pointed to the way in which God can in righteousness bless the sinner that believes, but the law and the prophets were only the witnesses of good things to come. The righteousness of God is now *manifested*. It is now made manifest that God is in righteousness proclaiming the forgiveness of sins to the sinner, and justifying the ungodly that believe in Jesus.

Verses 22-23

This righteousness of God is 'toward' (N.Tr.) us in blessing, not against us in judgement as the natural heart would think. Moreover, it is 'towards all'. It is not confined to the Jew, nor is it simply towards believers, or the elect; it is towards all.

Only those, however, who have faith — the 'faith of Jesus Christ' — receive the blessing that the righteousness of God brings. Thus while the righteousness of God is 'toward all', it is only 'upon all those that believe'. The righteousness of God takes effect, or acts upon such. God,

Himself, apart from our experiences acts righteously in justifying the one that believes, from every charge.

What then is this believing, or 'faith of Jesus Christ', of which this verse speaks? God presents Christ, as a living Person, as an object for the faith of men; as one has said 'Jesus Christ is a divine Reality; and the 'faith of Jesus Christ' is simply that He becomes a Reality to the heart of the believer'. In the gospel Christ is presented in all the glory of His Person — His moral worth, His suitability to the sinner, His availability for all, and His accessibility to any needy soul. He is presented in connection with the glory of His work as dying on the Cross, 'offering Himself without spot to God'. He is presented as risen, ascended and in the glory of God, accepted by God to the entire satisfaction of God. To the one who believes, Jesus — a living Person in the glory — is all, and has done all, that is needed to meet God's holy nature, in order that God may righteously proclaim forgiveness toward all, and pronounce the one that believes justified. Thus the apostle preaches, 'Through this man is preached unto you the forgiveness of sins: and by Him all that believe are justified from all things' (Acts 13:38-39). If then the proclamation of forgiveness goes out in righteousness toward all, it is because all need it. Whatever other differences there may be between men, there is no difference in this respect that 'all have sinned, and come short of the glory of God'.

VERSE 24

While all have come short, those who believe are 'justified freely by His grace, through the redemption that is in Christ Jesus'. It has been pointed out that this word translated 'freely' is, in John 15:25, translated 'without a cause'. Men hated Christ without a cause, as far as He was concerned; and God justifies the believer in Jesus, without a cause as far as the believer is concerned. While it is an act done in absolute consistency with God's nature; it is an act of pure grace towards the believer. The believer is justified righteously and freely.

To be justified means that the believer is completely cleared from every charge of guilt before God. And being cleared by God, Himself, it follows that no question of the believer's sins will ever be raised by God. If God has righteously justified the believer from his sins, it follows that God could not righteously raise the question of his sins again. The very righteousness that has dealt with the sins of the believer prevents the question of his sins being raised again.

If, however, God is able to justify the believer in righteousness and grace, there must be some adequate ground for God to thus act. This is now brought before us; it 'is through the redemption that is in Christ Jesus'. Redemption is the act which, through the payment of a price, frees the sinner from all the liabilities under which he has failed. Redemption does a great deal more than set us free from our sins; it includes the setting free of the body from death and disease, and this involves a body of glory like Christ's. Redemption in its fullness frees from guilt, judgement, death, and the power of the enemy, and brings us back to God in glory, with and like Christ. In that glory, when the work of redemption is complete, the assembled hosts will say to Christ 'Thou are worthy ... for Thou hast *redeemed* us to God by Thy blood' (Revelation 5:9).

Redemption is brought into this passage to show that justification is part of that great work of redemption which ultimately sets us with Christ and like Christ in glory. Justification is included in redemption, but redemption covers a great deal more than justification. Redemption sets the believer free from every single thing by which Satan has any claim against us, or any power over us. The Israelites were not only screened from the destroying angel by the blood on the door posts in Egypt, but they were also brought out of Egypt by the passage of the Red Sea, and thus were entirely delivered from the power of Pharaoh. Justification is the first part of this great redemption. As believers we are not only forgiven, but we are justified — we are set free from all title Satan can have against us on account of our sins.

This redemption is 'In Christ Jesus'. We see our justification set forth in Him. It is our privilege to see that we are as clear from every charge as He is; but we see more, we see all that we shall be, as the result of redemption in its fullness, set forth in Christ Jesus in the glory.

VERSES 25-26

If, moreover, God redeems His people, it is evident that He has the right of redemption. Satan was allowed to enter the garden, and man fell from God to the devil. God, however, never gave up His sovereign right to redeem man from the power of the devil. Nevertheless, the right to redeem can only be exercised by the payment of a price. For the peace of our souls God has clearly set forth the ground on which He exercises His rights of redemption. Thus at once our eyes are directed to Christ Jesus and His work, 'Whom God has set forth a mercy seat through faith in His blood' (N.Tr.). We do well to give good heed to this great statement, as it presents the death of Christ in all its unchanging efficacy under the eye of God as the sure ground of our justification and redemption. It is the great central truth of the chapter on which all blessing is based.

Three Old Testament Scriptures will give us the leading truths of the mercy seat. First Exodus 25:17 tells us the mercy seat was of *'pure gold'*. This speaks to us of the glory of the Person of Christ. He is a divine Person — God manifest in the flesh. Second, Exodus 26:34 tells us the mercy seat was put upon the ark *'in the most holy place'*. The most holy place was a picture of heaven itself. (Hebrews 9:24). It speaks of where Christ is today in the presence of God. Third, Leviticus 16:14-15 tells us that the blood of the sacrifice was brought within the veil — into the most holy place — and sprinkled *'upon the mercy seat'*. This speaks, not only of the work of Christ, but of God's acceptance of that work. Thus in the mercy seat, as presented in these three Scriptures, we have brought before us the glory of the Person of Christ, the glory of the place that He is in, and the glory of the work that He has done. We learn Who He is, where He is, and what He has done for the satisfaction of God.

Thus Christ Jesus 'set forth as a mercy seat through faith in His blood' means that faith sees that Christ, in the glory of His Person and the preciousness of His work, is ever before God. No creature will ever know the infinite glory of His Person, or the infinite value of His blood; but faith rests in God's appreciation of His Person and work. The basis of all peace in the soul is the knowledge that Christ, in the glory of His Person, and the efficacy of His work is ever before God and fully accepted by God. Faith does not look within to try and find some rest in our appreciation of Christ and His work. Faith looks without to Christ in the glory and rests on God's appreciation of His worth and His precious blood.

To have true rest and peace we must rest in that about which the devil can raise no question, and therefore that which is outside ourselves and our changing feelings and experiences. We can alone find this resting place for the soul in Christ in the glory and God's eternal satisfaction in His precious blood. One has truly said, 'Faith in Christ's work is not our accepting it, gladly as we do, but believing God has' (J.N.Darby).

To faith's view, of God's acceptance of the blood, it becomes clear how God was righteous in having borne with the Old Testament saints, when they sinned. His forbearance was seen at the time: His righteousness in forbearing is revealed now. So too, at the present time, God is seen to be just, while justifying the believer in Jesus. It is not simply that God is just in spite of justifying the believer in Jesus; but God is just *in justifying*. God justifies righteously.

Thus on the ground of the precious blood of Christ, which is ever before God in all its value, the righteousness of God is towards all proclaiming to all the forgiveness of sins; and the righteousness of God takes effect upon all that believe in clearing such from all their sins.

VERSES 27-28

All boasting on our part is shut out. If our blessing entirely depends upon the work of another, the report of which we have received by faith, it is evident that we have nothing in which to boast as if by our works we had secured the blessing. Therefore, says the apostle, we reach the conclusion, 'That a man is justified by faith without the deeds of the law'.

VERSES 29-30

Moreover, justification is clearly not confined to the Jew. Seeing there is 'one God' who justifies the circumcised Jew on the principle of faith, as well as the uncircumcised

Gentile by faith, it is evident that God is acting towards all in righteousness and grace.

Verse 31

Does then justification by faith, which shuts out the law as a means of blessing, make the law of none effect? On the contrary, the justification of the believer on the ground of the precious blood establishes the law. The real purpose for which the law was given was to convict men of sin; and, for this purpose, the law is still effectual. In this chapter the apostle has been using the law to convict all the world of their guilt, and has thus established the truth of the law.

4.   THE POWER OF GOD IN JUSTIFYING

CHAPTER 4

In chapter three we have seen *the righteousness of God* set forth in a twofold way; first, in proclaiming forgiveness to all; secondly, in justifying the sinner that believes in Jesus and His blood. In chapter four we see *the power of God* in setting the believer before Himself beyond judgement and death, and therefore beyond the power of Satan — by delivering Christ for our offences and raising Him from among the dead.

The blood of Christ is before us in chapter three, the resurrection of Christ in chapter four. One witnesses to the righteousness of God; the other to the power of God.

Very blessedly the chapter sets forth the righteous condition in which God reckons the believer to be before Himself. In the sixth chapter we shall come to our reckoning; in this chapter we have God's reckoning. This is of the first importance, for we need, above all else, to know how God views the one that believes in Jesus. It will be noticed that this word 'reckon' occurs eleven times in the chapter. Twice it is translated 'counted' (verses 3, 5); six times it is translated 'imputed' (verses 6, 8, 11, 22, 23, 24); and three times 'reckoned' (verses 4, 9, 10). In the original language it is the same word and on each occasion should be translated 'reckoned'. Verses 6 and 24, show plainly that, in this chapter, it is God that reckons. It helps us to see that it is not a question of what men may reckon the believer to be, or even what the believer may reckon himself to be, but wholly a question of what God reckons the believer to be. What gives solid peace is to see that God reckons the believer to be before Him in a righteous condition, beyond death, judgement, and the power of Satan, as set forth in Christ risen. Then, indeed, it is our privilege, as believers, to reckon with God about ourselves.

Further it is of importance to distinguish between righteousness, as brought before us in chapter three, and the righteousness spoken of in chapter four. Chapter three speaks of 'the righteousness of God', chapter four of the 'righteousness of faith', an expression that occurs in verses 11 and 13. The righteousness of God is, as we have seen, God's own righteousness, or God acting righteously in proclaiming forgiveness to all, and in justifying the believer. In this chapter the apostle unfolds before us the result of God having justified those that believe in Jesus and His blood. He shows that such are viewed by God as in a *righteous condition*. Thus 'the righteousness of faith' is that righteous condition in which the believer is seen before God. It is not only that God has acted righteously in justifying the believer, but that the believer who is justified by God is in a righteous condition as cleared from every charge of guilt. Thus while chapter three brings before us the righteous way in which God acts, chapter four brings before us the righteous condition in which the believer is seen by God.

THE RIGHTEOUSNESS OF FAITH ILLUSTRATED (4:1-5)
VERSES 1-3

The apostle turns to the history of Abraham to illustrate the righteous condition in which God views the believer. Every Jew would boast in Abraham as the one from whom he was descended by natural birth. If then justification by faith can be proved in the case of Abraham it would naturally arrest the Jew as an argument of great weight. Now Scripture definitely states that Abraham was justified. How then was he justified? Was it by works? If so, says the apostle, he has whereof to boast, but not before God. The apostle then appeals to Scripture to tell us how Abraham was justified. He asks, 'what saith the Scripture'? The answer given by Scripture is that 'Abraham believed God and it was reckoned unto him as righteousness' (N.Tr.).

The Scripture referred to is the great scene described in Genesis 15, when the Lord appeared to Abraham in a vision. Abraham was told to 'Look now toward heaven, and tell the stars, if thou be able to number them'. As he looks he has to listen to what God says, 'so shall thy seed be'. He looked, he listened, and he believed; and God counted it to him as righteousness. As we read 'He believed in the Lord; and he counted it to him for righteousness' (Genesis 15:6). Apart from any works, simply by believing, he was reckoned by God to be in a righteous condition.

In the same way today, the sinner's gaze is directed to the heavens, and to Christ in the glory, and as he looks he listens to God expressing His delight and satisfaction with Christ and His work. He hears God telling him that the blood is on the mercy seat ever before His eye; or, in other words, that such is the efficacy of the work of Christ that is ever before God, that He can justify the one that believes. The sinner that believes is justified, or reckoned to be in a righteous condition before God. Moreover this righteous condition is set forth in Christ in the glory. As a sinner my gaze is directed to Christ in the glory to see God's satisfaction with the blood; as a believer my gaze is directed to Christ in the glory to see set forth in Him the righteous condition in which I am set before God.

VERSES 4-5

Had Abraham been justified by his works, his justification would have been due to him because of what he had done, even as wages are due to the workman. There would have been no question of grace on God's side or faith on Abraham's. But in justifying, God acts in pure grace; for let us not forget that the believer in himself is 'ungodly'. Thus the righteous condition in which God views the believer, is the result of pure grace that does not look for, or recognise, any merit in the person justified. This is a very blessed and establishing truth for the believer. On the one hand it presents God as acting in all the love and grace of His heart, on the ground of what Christ has done; on the other hand, it relieves the believer from any disturbing thought that after all this righteous condition is the result of anything that he has done or can do.

THE RIGHTEOUSNESS OF FAITH DESCRIBED (4:6-8)

If the righteous condition in which the believer is viewed is illustrated in the case of Abraham, the blessedness of it is described in David. David is said to describe the blessedness of the man to whom God reckons righteousness without works. Psalm 32:1-2 is quoted to describe this blessedness. David does not directly say anything about the believer being reckoned to be in a righteous condition, but simply says, 'Blessed are they whose iniquities are forgiven and whose sins are covered. Blessed is the man to whom the Lord will not reckon sin'. It is clear then that not to have sin reckoned is, in other words, to be reckoned to be in a righteous condition. God would have every believer to know the blessedness of this in his own soul.

THE RIGHTEOUSNESS OF FAITH SEPARATES FROM THE WORLD (4:9-12)

Abraham illustrates the way the believer acquires the righteousness of faith; David describes the blessedness of it. However, both Abraham and David belonged to the circumcision. Is then this blessedness confined to Israel, or the circumcision? To answer this question, the apostle once again appeals to the history of Abraham. The sign of circumcision was the great distinguishing mark between Israel and the Gentiles. When was Abraham reckoned righteous? Was it when he was an uncircumcised man like the rest of the Gentiles, or was it a blessing that he received after he was separated from the Gentiles by the rite of circumcision? Clearly it was when he was uncircumcised, hence the blessing is free for the uncircumcised Gentile today, as well as to the circumcised Jew.

Moreover, circumcision was given as the 'seal of the righteousness of the faith which he had yet being uncircumcised'. This surely indicates that the one reckoned to be in a righteous condition before God must henceforth refuse the activities of the flesh. If he is in a righteous condition before God; he must walk in a righteous way before men. Righteousness of faith before God will put a 'seal' or stamp upon a man which will be expressed in a life before men that refuses the flesh and its evil. This refusal of the flesh, we know, can only be in the power of the Spirit who is given to those who believe. Separation from the world and a walk in practical righteousness will be the outcome of being in a righteous condition before God.

Thus Abraham is said to be 'the father of all them that believe', and 'the father of circumcision' to all believers who walk in the steps of Abraham. As 'the father of all that believe' he sets forth the righteous condition in which the believer is viewed by God. As 'the father of circumcision' he sets forth the holy and separate walk that becomes those who are reckoned righteous.

THE RIGHTEOUSNESS OF FAITH IN VIEW OF THE WORLD TO COME (4:13-16)

VERSE 13

In connection with the 'righteousness of faith' there comes into view the prospect of an inheritance in the world to come. The one who is reckoned to be in a righteous condition, is not only separate from the flesh and the world, as set forth in circumcision, but, has opened up before him a glorious inheritance. The circumcision of Abraham would teach the believer that he is not justified in order to take a place in this world; while 'the promise' to Abraham tells us that we are justified in view of an inheritance of glory in the world to come.

To set forth this great truth the apostle again turns to Abraham's history and speaks of the promise of the inheritance. This promise was made, or renewed to Abraham, on the same day that he was reckoned to be righteous, as we read in Genesis 15: 18 'In the same day the Lord made a covenant with Abram, saying, unto thy seed have I given this land'. This promise of the inheritance was given long before the law, and in no wise depended upon works of law.

VERSES 14-15

If the blessings of the promise could only be obtained by keeping the law, two results would follow:–

First, faith would become vain, and secondly, the promise would be made of none effect, for it is evident that none have kept the law. Seeing all have transgressed the law, so far from bringing blessing it works wrath, for it condemns the transgressor. Had there been no law there would have been no transgression. The word does not say 'no sin'. Transgression is disobedience to a known law. It makes manifest the presence of sin, the principle of which is lawlessness, or doing one's own will in spite of all legal restraint.

VERSE 16

The truth, however, is that the blessing of the inheritance is reached on the principle of faith, that it might be given to us wholly of grace. This makes the inheritance sure to all who are in the line of faith of which Abraham is the father; whether by natural birth they be Israelites or Gentiles.

Abraham is thus seen to be the father of all to whom righteousness is reckoned on the principle of faith (verse 11); the father of all the justified who walk in true separation to God (verse 12); and the father of all that inherit the promises by grace on the principle of faith (verse 16).

THE POWER OF GOD THAT PERFORMS WHAT GOD HAS PROMISED (4:17-25)

The glorious inheritance that is opened up to those who are justified entails the power of God that will bring the believer into the inheritance. This mighty power is seen in resurrection, which sets forth the power of God over death — not merely the power to prevent a man dying, but the far greater power that raises a man that is dead.

Again the apostle turns to the history of Abraham to illustrate the power of God in resurrection, as well as the believer's faith in the power of God. God had justified Abraham, separated him from the world, and given him the promise of a glorious inheritance; but, as a matter of fact, death stood between the justified Abraham and the inheritance of glory. His body was dead; as far as having a child was concerned, Sarah's body was dead. All were under death, but Abraham's faith believed in the power of God over death. He believed that God was able to perform what He had promised through resurrection power.

Abraham was called to believe in the power of God that can raise the dead. The believer today is called to believe in the power of God that *has raised the dead,* for this mighty power has been put forth in the resurrection of Jesus our Lord. Already we have seen *the righteousness of God* that is toward all the ungodly, *the grace of God* that righteously justifies the ungodly that believe; now we have *the power of God* that will bring the justified into the glorious inheritance.

This power has been set forth in Jesus Christ, our Lord, who was delivered to death and judgement for our offences, and has been raised from the dead for our justification. In that blessed Risen Man we see set forth *the righteous condition* in which we are before God; *the glory* into which we shall be brought, and *the power* which will bring us into the glory.

As we look at Christ risen we see One that is absolutely clear of all the offences that He bore upon the cross. One who is before God in absolute purity, whiter than snow. One against whom no one can bring a charge. His condition sets forth the righteous condition in which God views the believer — the righteousness of faith. In God's reckoning the believer is before Him even as Christ is.

The third of Romans sets forth the great propitiatory work of Christ, on the ground of which God can righteously proclaim forgiveness of sins unto all. This chapter presents the substitutionary work of Christ whereby all the believer's sins have been dealt with. The question of our sins has been settled *by God*, through the work of Christ, and therefore to the entire satisfaction of God. It was God Who delivered up Christ; it was for our sins God delivered Him up; it was to judgement that God delivered Him. The sins being borne and the judgement exhausted, it was God who raised Christ from the dead to set forth in the risen Christ how completely the believer is cleared from sins, and judgement, and the penalty of death.

Do we hesitate to believe what God says because of what we find in ourselves, or because of the greatness of the blessing. Then let us learn by Abraham's simple faith, of which three things are stated.

First, 'he considered not his own body'. He did not look at himself and say — that cannot be true because of what I am (verse 19).

Secondly, 'he staggered not at the promise of God through unbelief'. He did not doubt or limit the grace of God and say — 'this is too good to be true'.

Thirdly, he was 'fully persuaded' that what God had promised He was able to perform.

So with the believer. He can say, 'I see Christ is everything, and has done everything that God requires, in order that the grace of God may proclaim the forgiveness of sins to me, and I know that God Himself has justified me, reckoning me to be before Himself in the righteous condition that Christ is in; beyond judgement, death and the power of Satan'. Turning from self and all that we are, looking at Christ risen, and listening to what God says about Christ, we too shall be 'fully persuaded'.

5. THE LOVE OF GOD ADMINISTERING BLESSING THROUGH OUR LORD JESUS CHRIST

CHAPTER 5:1-11

The opening verses of chapter five present a summing up of the truths unfolded in the early part of the epistle. The apostle has brought before us the righteousness of God in proclaiming forgiveness to all, and in justifying the believer (3:22, 25-26); the grace of God in blessing the ungodly (3:23-24; 4:4, 16); and the power of God in raising the dead and setting the believer before Himself as clear of all sins and judgement as the risen Christ.

Now we learn that *the love of God* is behind all His ways in righteousness, grace and power. Moreover all the blessings that the love of God has secured for believers come to them 'through' or 'by' our Lord Jesus Christ. It is 'through' Him we have peace with God (verse 1); 'by' Him we have access into favour (verse 2); 'by' His blood we are justified, and 'by' Him we shall be saved from wrath (verse 9); we are reconciled unto God 'by' the death of His Son; we shall be saved from present evil 'by' His life and 'through' our Lord Jesus Christ we also joy in our God, 'by' whom we have now received the reconciliation (verse 11).

Two main themes pass before us in this summary of Christian blessing: first, the position and portion of the believer before God in view of the coming glory (verses 1-2): secondly, the experiences and blessings of the believer while journeying through this present world (verses 3-11).

THE POSITION AND PORTION OF THE BELIEVER BEFORE GOD (5:1-2)

VERSES 1-2

The latter part of chapter 4 (verses 17-25) asserts the great truth that believers are justified in order that they may be suited to have part in a scene of glory beyond the power of death. Our suitability for this coming glory is set forth in Jesus risen from among the dead. If our Lord Jesus Christ 'gave Himself for our sins', it was not that we might be relieved from the burden of sin in order to enjoy this present scene, but, that 'He might deliver us out of this present evil world'. We are justified in view of having part in what Scripture speaks of as 'the world to come' (Hebrews 2:5). This 'world to come', or millennial age, will be introduced by the coming of the Lord Jesus, Who will put down all lawlessness, and introduce a reign of blessing marked by righteousness, peace and joy (Romans 14:17). Psalm 72 very blessedly sets before us this coming reign of Christ. There we learn that in the day of His reign, Christ will judge the people *with righteousness*. The result being 'the mountains shall bring *peace* to the people', and there will be 'abundance of *peace* so long as the moon endureth'. Righteousness and peace will lead to *joy*, for we read, that 'daily shall He be praised', and 'all nations shall call Him blessed'.

The One Who is going to introduce the Kingdom is risen and enthroned in glory. Believers, owning the Lordship of Christ, come under His sway even now, and thus anticipate in their spirits the blessings of the coming Kingdom, marked by righteousness, peace and joy in the Holy Spirit. These opening verses set before us these blessings that belong to the justified who come under the present dominion of our Lord Jesus Christ. 'Being justified by faith we have peace with God through our Lord Jesus Christ: by whom also we have access by faith into this favour wherein we stand, and rejoice in hope of the glory of God'. Here then we have the righteousness, peace and joy that will mark the coming Kingdom, presented as the present portion of the believer. What will be known outwardly in the Kingdom is to be known and enjoyed in the heart of the believer today.

All these blessings are 'through our Lord Jesus Christ'. Looking from self to Christ we see in Him One that is absolutely clear of all our offences, and the judgement they entailed. We see there is nothing between God and Christ, consequently there is nothing between God and the believer. This gives peace toward God. Peace within is the result of seeing that peace has been made without. The One who went into the storm of Calvary is now in the calm of the glory. At the cross Christ met, for the believer, every enemy; and every enemy that He met He vanquished, for He is risen and in glory; the result is peace with God.

Again we look to Jesus and see that He is in all the unclouded favour of God, and into this favour the believer has access. Then again we see in Him One Who is perfectly suited to the glory of God, and in the glory, and for this glory, He has suited the believer: 'We rejoice in hope of the glory of God'.

Thus, in Christ, we see set forth the blessed position in which the believer stands before God; justified from every charge, in the everlasting favour of God, and suited for the glory of God for which he waits in hope.

THE BLESSINGS AND EXPERIENCE OF THE BELIEVER IN PASSING THROUGH THIS PRESENT WORLD (5:3-11)
VERSE 3

While hope looks on to the coming glory, as to fact, the believer is still in a world of sin, and sorrow, and death. The verses that follow present the experiences and blessings of believers while passing through such a world. If justification fits us for the world to come, in which the glory of God will be displayed, it also sets us apart from this present evil world in which man seeks his own glory without any thought of the will of God.

Passing through this world the believer must of necessity meet with tribulation which calls for endurance, leads to experience, and quickens hope. Seeing the world had manifested its hostility to God, the Lord Jesus warned His disciples that, 'In the world ye shall have tribulation' (John 16:33). Again the apostle warned young converts, 'that we must through much tribulation enter into the Kingdom of God' (Acts 14:22). The tribulation will doubtless take different forms at different times, and in different cases, but all true believers will have to face trial.

Nevertheless, God intends that the tribulation we may pass through shall turn to our spiritual blessing. Therefore, the apostle adds, 'We glory in tribulations also: knowing that tribulation worketh endurance'. He does not suggest that we glory in tribulation as such, but because it works to our spiritual advantage. Tribulation leads to endurance. In the light of what is coming we learn to endure what is present. Our Lord has been before us in this path. Walking in the light of the glory that was before Him, He endured the trials He had to meet; as we read,

'Who for the joy that was set before Him *endured* the cross, despising the shame'; and again we read, He 'endured such contradiction of sinners against Himself'. Truly, in His case, the trial drew forth the perfection of the endurance that He had; in ours we have to *learn* endurance. Rejoicing in hope of the glory we, too, shall be able to endure in the midst of tribulations. Losing sight of the glory we shall be in danger, in the presence of trial, of giving up rather than enduring.

Verse 4

The result of enduring in tribulation is that we gain experience*. Endurance leads to a practical proof of the reality of the care and interest of God in preserving and keeping the soul in tribulation. Thus, in tribulation, we gain an experimental acquaintance with God; we practically prove the grace, tender sympathy, and mercy of our God.

Moreover, the experience of the goodness of God in the midst of trials strengthens 'hope' in the soul. We look outside and beyond this world of trial to the rest that remaineth in the world to come, though at present we only possess that home of glory in hope. But hope makes the future glory a present reality.

Verse 5

Furthermore, the Christian's hope maketh not ashamed. The failure of the earthly hope in which men may boast oftentimes makes them ashamed of their hope. The hope of the Christian is sure because connected with the love of

---

* The word 'experience' means 'practical proof'. It is used in five other Scriptures. In 2 Corinthians 2:9; 13:3 and Philippians 2:22 it is translated 'proof'. In 2 Corinthians 8:2 'trial' and in 2 Corinthians 9:13 'experiment' ('proof', N.Tr.). The connection in all these Scriptures shows that the word signifies learning by practical proof.

God shed abroad in our hearts. Faith realises that our hope is certain seeing that the glory for which we hope is secured by a love that will never fail. Already, the apostle has brought before us the righteousness of God, and the grace of God in chapter 3; the power of God in resurrection in chapter 4; now we have the love of God made real to our hearts by the Holy Ghost given to us. 'The only begotten Son which is in the bosom of the Father, He hath declared Him'. Only a Divine Person is great enough to reveal the heart of the Father; and, when revealed, only another Divine Person — the Holy Spirit — is great enough to make that love a reality to our hearts.

VERSE 6

At once, however, the Holy Spirit turns our thoughts to the cross for the expression of that love. The love is made good in our hearts; but we are not left to look within our hearts to find an expression of that love. That death which is the witness of God's righteousness in chapter 3, and of God's power in chapter 4, is now brought forward as the witness of God's love in chapter 5.

VERSE 7

To set forth the greatness of this love we are reminded that it was when we were 'without strength', and 'ungodly' that Christ died for us. When we were utterly helpless, unable to do anything for God, and ungodly, unwilling to do anything for God, then it was that love made the great sacrifice by dying for us.

In the days of old, the prophet, writing to Israel, reminds them of the love of God. He likens Israel to a newborn, helpless babe 'cast out in the open field', and left to perish with no eye to pity and no heart to have compassion. Then says Jehovah, *'thy time was the time of love'*. Man's time of need was God's time of love (Ezekiel 16:1-14). So our time of helplessness and ungodliness was God's time of love.

To emphasise this love, a contrast is drawn between the way men act and the way that the love of God has taken. Amongst men there would scarcely be found a man who would die for *a righteous man*; though it is possible that, moved by some strong impulse, one might be found daring enough to die for *a good man*. But where is there a love amongst men that would lead anyone to die for *a sinner*? In contrast to all that can be found amongst men, 'God commends His love, in that while we were yet sinners Christ died for us'.

VERSES 9-10

Salvation is another great blessing that follows from being justified. There is wrath coming on the ungodly, but believers can say, 'we shall be saved from wrath by Him'. The Lord Jesus is 'our deliverer from the coming wrath' (1 Thessalonians 1:10). He will take us out of the scene of judgement before the judgement falls.

Moreover, the justified man is also reconciled. Not only did we love sins and lusts, but we positively hated God. Our wicked works had alienated us from God (Colossians 1:21). Justification clears away our guilt; reconciliation removes the enmity in our hearts and makes us so suited to God that He can view us with Divine complacency. The death of Christ which declares the righteousness of God by which we are justified, also discloses the love of God by which we are reconciled; the knowledge of the love of God removes the enmity to God.

A further blessing is, that 'being reconciled, we shall be saved by His life'. Here we have the present aspect of salvation. Not only are we saved from wrath to come, but we are saved from the evils and dangers of this present world by His life. As we read in another passage 'He is able also to save them to the uttermost that come unto God by Him, seeing He ever liveth to make intercession for them' (Hebrews 7:25).

VERSE 11

The blessed result is that the believer is brought to 'boast in God through our Lord Jesus Christ, by whom we have now received the reconciliation' (N.Tr.). Through the Lord Jesus Christ — all that He is, all that He has done, and all that is set forth in Him — we realise it is God's delight to have us before Him in perfect suitability to Himself.

Thus in this great summing up of the first portion of the epistle, the believer, as he passes through this present world on the way to glory, is viewed as:–

1   Making spiritual progress through tribulations;

2   With the love of God shed abroad in his heart by the Holy Ghost;

3   Justified by the blood of Christ;

4   Knowing that he will be saved from the coming wrath;

5   Reconciled to God by the death of His Son;

6   Saved from every opposing evil by the One who is ever living for us;

7   Joying in God through our Lord Jesus Christ.

DIVISION 2

CHRIST THE HEAD OF A NEW RACE AND THE BLESSINGS OF THOSE IN CHRIST

Chapters 5:12 – 8

1. INTRODUCTORY

The first division of the epistle presents the blessings that have been secured to the believer *through* Christ. This second division unfolds the blessings that belong to the believer *in* Christ. It presents our new position in Christ, in contrast to our old position in Adam. As natural men we are connected with Adam and involved in the fall and its consequences. As believers we are connected with Christ, and share in the blessings that belong to His line.

In the first part of the epistle the question of our sins and guilt is dealt with; in this second division the question of our state is taken up. The apostle no longer speaks of what we have *done*, but of what we *are*; not of the bad fruit, but of the bad tree that produced the fruit.

The first exercises of an awakened soul are generally concerned with the sins that have been committed and the judgement involved. When these questions are settled there arises another difficulty to trouble the soul, which, at the outset of our Christian career was hardly, if at all, suspected. We discover that, though we have a new nature, with new desires after Christ and the things of God, there is still in us the old nature, dominated by an evil principle which God calls sin. Moreover, we find that this old nature seeks to assert itself in its lusts in opposition to the will of God. Further we find that this old nature with its lusts is too strong for us. In this fresh portion of the epistle there is unfolded before us the way of practical deliverance, from the dominion of sin and all that sin entails, so that we may enjoy, in the power of the Holy Spirit, the blessings of the delivered soul.

The truth is presented in the following order:

First, Christ is brought before us as the new Head of a new race, with the presentation of the blessing that belong to those in His line (chapter 5:12-21).

Secondly, we are shown the way of deliverance from the power of sin (chapter six).

Thirdly, we learn the way of deliverance from law (chapter seven).

Fourthly, we learn the way of deliverance from the flesh, and the blessings that are enjoyed in the power of the Spirit (chapter eight).

2.   CHRIST THE HEAD OF A NEW RACE
Chapter 5:12-21

Seeing that this fresh division of the epistle sets forth the position, and blessing, that belong to the believer as being before God 'in Christ', it naturally commences by bringing before us Christ as the Head of a new race. We learn from this passage that as we were identified with Adam and the sorrowful consequences that follow from all in his line; so, as believers, we are identified with Christ and share in the blessings that are the portion of those in His line.

We shall learn that we have been identified with Christ in His death to close up our links with Adam and his race; and that we have been identified with Christ in resurrection to share in all the blessings that belong to His race.

Verse 12

The passage opens by tracing all the sorrows that have come into this world to one man — Adam. Through Adam's act of disobedience sin came into the world, and death by sin, and so death passed upon all Adam's race. The outcome of 'sin' must be sins, but it is of 'sin' that the apostle more especially speaks in this portion of the epistle. In chapters 1 to 5 verse 11 the word sin occurs but twice; in this division, chapter 5 verse 12 to chapter 8, it occurs thirty-four times. 'Sin' is the evil principle of 'law-lessness', or the creature doing his own will. This evil principle entered the world through Adam's one act of disobedience. Death followed as the penalty of sin. Sins can be forgiven; but 'sin', the evil principle which leads to sins, can only be met by death that brings to an end the life governed by sin. Therefore the penalty of sin is death. Thus the death penalty passed upon all Adam's race. That all have come under the evil principle of sin is proved by the fact that all have sinned. The bad fruit shows the character of the tree. So the apostle says, 'death passed upon all men, for that all have sinned'.

In verse 18 the apostle continues his teaching by showing the blessings that come to those in Christ's line. First, however, in verses 13-17, which form a parenthesis, he presses three truths:–

Firstly, that the evil principle of sin existed apart altogether from law.

Secondly, that Adam was a figure of Christ the Head of a new race.

Thirdly, that as Adam's sin affected the whole of his race; so, much more, what Christ has done benefits the whole of His race.

VERSES 13-14

First, as to law. It is evident that Adam was put under law — in his case a very simple law forbidding him to eat of a certain tree. 2,500 years later the law was given to Israel through Moses. But, between Adam and Moses there was no specific law forbidding this or that. The question then arises: Can man be condemned for doing that which is not forbidden? The answer is that sin is not put to man's account, as actual transgression of a known law, where no law exists. Nevertheless, though not charged with transgressing when there is no law, it is evident that man does his own will and in consequence suffers the penalty of death. This is proved by the fact that death reigned from Adam to Moses. It is thus proved that Adam's race is under sin and the penalty of death apart altogether from law and the transgression of the law.

Secondly, in this parenthesis, we learn there is another Head of another race of whom Adam was only 'the figure'. Christ is presented as the Head of a new race. The consideration of all that came in through Adam helps us to understand the blessing that has come in through Christ.

VERSES 15-17

Thirdly, the effect of grace through Christ far surpasses the effect of sin through Adam. The surpassing character of this grace is proved in a threefold way:–

First, in verse 15 we learn that the grace of God abounds over the offence of Adam. If the offence of one man, Adam, brings death upon his race, much more the grace of God brings the gift of life, in grace, by one Man, Jesus Christ, to His line.

Secondly, in verse 16 we learn that the justification of God abounds over the judgement of God. The sentence of judgement that passed upon men was on account of one sin involving all in judgement; the grace of God takes account of 'many offences', not for judgement, but for justification.

Thirdly, in verse 17 we learn that life abounds over death. The apostle says, 'if by one man's offence death reigned by one; much more they which receive abundance of grace, and of the free gift of righteousness shall reign in life by one'. We might have thought that the contrast to 'death reigning' would be 'life reigning'. It is, however, more than this, for the word is 'They … shall reign in life'. This opens to the believer a wonderful vista of blessing. The time is coming when the saints will reign *with Christ*; now grace makes it possible for the saint to reign in life *by Christ*. It is God's thought that by Christ we should be made completely superior to the power of sin, lawlessness and self will. That in the power of a life sustained by Christ, we should overcome all evil whether in the flesh or the world.

What a victorious life this opens up to the believer! Instead of being constantly overcome by this evil principle — sin — so that sin reigns over us, there is set before us the blessed possibility of the believer reigning over sin by Jesus Christ. How this can be practically brought about is disclosed to us in chapters six, seven and eight, in which we have unfolded to us God's way of deliverance from sin, law, and the flesh. But before entering upon the experience and truth that leads to deliverance, God sets before us the blessed end to which it leads. In the future believers will reign in a world of blessing *with Christ*; now, in a world of sin and death, it is possible for them to reign in life *by Christ*, so that instead of being overcome by sin, the believer is an overcomer.

VERSE 18

Having, in this parenthesis, brought in Christ as the Head of His race, the apostle continues his argument from verse 12. There he had shown that through one man sin had entered into the world, and so death passed upon all men. Now he shows that the bearing of Christ's one act of righteousness is as wide as Adam's one act of disobedience. If Adam's act went out towards all men to condemnation; so the bearing of Christ's act is towards all men to justification of life. Unbelief may, alas, prevent that great act taking effect upon all, nonetheless, the blessing that act brings is for all. Justification of life is in contrast to the condemnation of death. The believer instead of being under the condemnation of death as the result of sin, comes under the justification of a life that is entirely free from sin. Instead of living a life that is dominated by sin and under the condemnation of death, he lives a life that is justified, or clear, from the power of sin and the death penalty.

VERSE 19

If the previous verse shows that the bearing of Christ's act is toward all, this verse shows that the actual application is limited to those in connection with Christ. By Adam's act of disobedience the many connected with him (that is to say, all men) are constituted sinners. By the obedience of Christ at the cross the many connected with Him (that is all believers) are constituted righteous.

VERSE 20

Moreover, the law made the offence abound. By forbidding sin it stirred up sin; and, moreover, it added to the evil of sin by making it transgression. Even so, where sin abounded grace did much more abound. Sin, by its reign of lawlessness, leads to death: grace, reigning through righteousness, or doing God's will, leads to eternal life. Here eternal life is viewed in its fullness in glory as the end of a course of righteousness, in contrast to death which lies at the end of a course of sin or lawlessness.

3.   DELIVERANCE FROM SIN

CHAPTER 6

The apostle has shown that Christ is the Head of a new race, and that through His one act of obedience grace brings justification and life to those in His line, so that they are able to reign in a life that is victorious over sin. To live this life it is necessary to be delivered from the dominance of sin. This then is the great subject of Romans six, the practical deliverance of the believer from the power of sin by being 'dead to sin'.

This subject is raised by the question, is the believer in his pathway through this world, to continue under the power of sin? The apostle answers this question with a decided 'No'; for, he says, 'Sin shall not have dominion over you' (verse 14). Moreover, he not only answers the question but also shows how the believer is delivered from the dominion of sin.

Before considering the chapter in detail it may be well to enquire, what is sin? And, what is involved in continuing in, or under the power of, sin? Sin is defined for us in the word of God as 'lawlessness' (1 John 3:4, N.Tr.) It is the evil principle of doing one's own will without reference to God, or, in other words, insubjection to God. By one man, Adam, this evil principle entered into the world; as a result, a system has grown up — called the world — which is entirely dominated by sin, or the will of man. The result of man doing his own will is depicted in Romans 3:9-19. It has filled the world with misery and sorrow and brought man under death and judgement. Moreover, what is true of the world as a whole is also true of each individual. The misery of each individual life arises from doing one's own will without reference to the will of God.

Turning from Adam to Christ we see a blessed and perfect Man who was in this world entirely free from the dominion of sin. The world He came into was governed by sin, or self will; Christ was governed by an entirely opposite principle — the principle of obedience or subjection to God's will. Coming into the world He had before Him the will of God, for He could say, 'Lo I come to do Thy will O God'. Passing through the world He could say, 'I seek not my own will, but the will of the Father which hath sent Me'; and again 'I do always those things that please Him' (John 5:30 and 8:29). Furthermore, in going out of the world He said, 'Not My will but Thine be done' (Luke 22:42). Thus, in Christ we see One who, from the beginning of His path to the end, wholly *lived to God.*

As we see this life set forth in Christ — the life lived to God — we see it in all its beauty and perfection, and thus seen it becomes very attractive to the believer. The *outward effects* of this life are brought before us in the Gospels where we see the Lord in contact with the world, and opposed by the flesh and the devil. The *inner blessedness* of this life, lived to God, is set before us in Psalm 16, which describes the path of life. There, set forth in Christ, we see, in all its beauty, a life lived wholly to God. We learn that it is a life of dependence upon the power of God, confidence in the love of God, and subjection to the will of God (verses 1-2); a life of lowliness that delights in the excellent of the earth (verse 3); that walks in separation from evil (verse 4); that knows satisfaction (verses 5-6); guidance (verse 7), support (verse 8) and joy (verses 9-11). As a result there never was a step taken in that life that had to be retraced, never an act to regret, never a thought to judge, or a word to recall.

Attracted by the beauty and blessedness of this life set forth in Christ the question arises, How can the believer be delivered from the dominion of sin, in order that he may live to God in this new life?

The answer in brief is, the believer can only be delivered from the power of sin by death to the man that is under sin, and can only live to God in this new life by the support of Christ, the living and risen Man who has died to sin and lives to God. In the beginning of Romans seven the figure of marriage is used to set forth this support.

DEAD TO SIN (6:1-2)
VERSES 1-2

The subject of death to sin is raised by the statement of the apostle, in the end of Romans five, that, 'where sin abounded grace did much more abound'. This statement at once leads the carnal mind to ask the foolish, if not wicked, question: 'Shall we continue in sin that grace may abound?' The apostle entirely repudiates this unholy suggestion. He will not allow that the believer, who is true to the position in which God has set the Christian, can continue living in sin.

The apostle, in the course of the chapter will show how the believer is dead to sin; but, at the outset he assumes that, in regard to sin, the only possible attitude for the believer to take is that he is 'dead to sin'. This being so, he asks, 'How shall we who have died to sin, still live in it?' His question does not suggest that we *ought not* to live in it, but that, having died to sin, we *cannot* live in it. The principle that underlies his assertion is plain and self evident, namely, we cannot die to something and at the same time live in it.

BAPTISM, AN ILLUSTRATION OF DEATH TO SIN (6:3-5)

Having in the first two verses set forth the great theme of the chapter — the believer's deliverance from the power of sin by death to sin — the apostle in verses 3-5 used baptism to illustrate the position of the believer as dead to sin.

VERSE 3

Those of us who have been baptised with a Christian baptism, i.e. baptised unto Jesus Christ — were baptised unto His death. We were, in the figure of baptism, identified with the death of Christ in order to have part down here in the position which His death sets us in relation to sin and the world. Baptism is a figure of death and burial. It is evident that *a dead man* has done with the life of self will in which he once lived, and *a buried man* has passed out of the sight of the world in which he once lived.

It is one thing, however, to pass out of the sight of the world and quite another to pass out of one's own sight; in other words, to see no man any more save Jesus only. The most difficult thing is to see oneself no more — to see the man that I was, a man that lived only for self, no more. When Christ was here there was nothing in common between His life and the life of the world. His life was entirely one of obedience to the Father's will, and of self denial in order to serve others in love. The life of the world is one of self will and self exaltation. By His death

Christ laid down the life to which, *in us*, sin attached; and by His burial He has passed out of sight of the world.

By baptism unto death we profess to have done with the life of the old man, to which sin attached, and, by burial we profess to have passed out of sight of a world dominated by sin.

VERSE 4

This, however, is a means to an end. Deliverance from a life of self will is in order that we may live a life of obedience to God; that is, that we may walk in newness of life to the glory of the Father. This life is set forth in Christ risen. If Christ has died to this world He has also been raised by the glory of the Father. 'Glory' displays what a person is. The glory of the Father sets forth all that the Father is. The Lord Jesus in His life, and at the cross, fully declared the Father in all His love, holiness, justice and power: having fully maintained the Father's glory it became a necessity of the Father's glory to raise Christ from the dead. All that the Father is demanded that the One who had maintained His glory should be raised from the dead.

Further, being raised from the dead by the glory of the Father expresses the great truth that Christ comes forth from the dead in a life that is perfectly suited to all that the Father is. In Christ risen we see a Man who lives to God in a life that is to the infinite satisfaction of the Father's heart.

When, however, it is said that this new life is set forth in Christ risen, the question may arise:

Did not Christ ever live to God? Personally, He most assuredly did, as we have seen set forth in perfection in Psalm 16. He perfectly lived to God in His life on earth, and He perfectly lives to God in resurrection. There is, however, this difference, in resurrection He lives to God as *having died to sin*, so that we, being delivered by His death, may also live to God. In resurrection He lives to God in a position which the believer can share with Him.

VERSE 5

This new life we live down here is after the pattern of the life of the risen Christ. If we have become identified with Christ in the likeness of His death, we shall be also in that of His resurrection. We are identified with His death to die to all that to which He died, and identified with His resurrection life to live to the pleasure of God. The apostle does not say that at present we are actually in the likeness of His resurrection, but that 'we shall be'. The full likeness of His resurrection involves our having bodies of glory like His own glorious body. But before we have the new bodies we have the new life which expresses itself in a new walk. The 'newness' of the life is seen in a walk that is entirely new to this world — a walk in obedience and subjection to the will of God.

DEATH WITH CHRIST (6:6-10)

VERSE 6

The apostle has referred to baptism to illustrate the truth that we have died with Christ. Now he comes to the great foundation fact, of which baptism is only a symbol. He says 'Our old man has been crucified with Him'. This is a fact that faith accepts on the authority of the word of God. Thus the apostle can speak of 'knowing' this. It is a fact that believers know by faith.

Our ordinary use of words may help us to understand the expression 'our old man'. We speak of 'the white man', and 'the black man'; but, in using such expressions, we do not refer to any particular individual. We refer to a race of men with certain characteristics; but seeing that all who compose the race have similar characteristics, the race can be described by an individual expression. So the expression 'old man' does not refer to any particular individual, it describes an order of man with certain characteristics. This order of man, we know, is Adam's fallen race, and the outstanding characteristic of that race is self-will. 'Our old man' is then an expression which describes all that we were morally as fallen men living a life of self will. In saying 'our old man' we recognise the old man is 'our' former self, or life.

This man that lives a life of self-will, caring nothing for God, will not do for God. To convince us of the hopeless character of this man God has fully tested the 'old man' under every possible test. He has been tried without law, under law, under priesthood, under royalty, and finally by the presence of Christ in grace. Under every test man has broken down proving that the old man is utterly evil, and that all hope of improving or reforming the 'old man' is useless. God has only one way of dealing with a man that is proved to be irremediably bad, that is by ending the life of the man in the judgement of death. Sins can be forgiven; but there can be no forgiveness for an evil nature, it can only be condemned and ended. Thus from the moment sin entered into the world God passed the sentence of death upon the man that was under sin. For the believer, this judgement has been carried out at the cross; so we can say, 'Our old man has been crucified with Him'. At the cross God dealt with the old man according to his deserts, and accordingly to God's own righteous demands. At the cross Christ vicariously represented before God 'our old man', so that when He was crucified we were crucified with Him. Not only did Christ bear our sins, but

He was made sin — made what we are. Thus our old man came up before God, and in His sight was judicially ended in the judgement of death. It becomes clear then that in this portion of the epistle it is no longer a question of Christ's death for us, but of our death with Christ.

Moreover our death with Christ not only meets the holy requirements of God, but has in view our practical walk. It was that 'the body of sin might be annulled that henceforth we should not serve sin'. Here the expression 'body of sin' refers to sin as a whole, in contrast to any particular manifestation of sin. We are apt to think of sin in connection with some particular failing to which we may be specially liable, and in which, in our case, the dominion of sin is most felt. Possibly we would be very well content to be set free from the dominion of sin in this special form. God, however, would have us free from the dominion of sin as a whole, not simply in part. This freedom can only be obtained on the ground that our old man that is under sin has been crucified with Christ. Sin, indeed, still exists, but can have no power over a corpse. Death annuls its power. The practical end is that being dead to sin we should no longer serve it.

VERSE 7

We are delivered by death from being servants to sin. It is clear that he that has died is justified from sin. A dead man has no longer an active will of his own. He can no longer be charged with self will.

VERSE 8

This however is not all. Death for the believer is the way into life. So, from speaking of death, the apostle now passes on to speak of life. He says, 'If we have died with Christ, we believe that we shall also *live* with Him'. In verse 9 he speaks of Christ 'being *raised* from the dead', and in verse 10 he says, 'in that Christ *liveth*, He *liveth* unto God'. Obviously that life is the subject of these verses. Looking into the future the apostle sets before us the full and glorious result of having died with Christ. 'If', says he, 'we have died with Christ, we believe that we shall also *live with Him*'. Who can apprehend the blessedness that lies behind these words, 'live with Him'. We know the grace of our Lord Jesus Christ, that He became poor and *lived with us*, full of grace and truth. That however, was only a means to an end; the glorious end being that we should *live with Him*.

Verse 9

Nor is this all, we shall not only live with Him, but we shall live where He lives in the resurrection sphere. This is a region where death hath no more dominion.

Verse 10

Furthermore, we shall not only 'live with Him', and live where He lives, but we shall *live as He lives*. Verse 10 tells us how He lives. Having died to sin, 'He liveth unto God'. The resurrection sphere is a scene in which God is all in all. God is all as the One who fills the vision, and God is all as the source and spring of every thought and affection that goes out to God in worship and adoration. This, indeed, will be living to God. It is true that personally Christ ever lived to God in His pathway through this world; but while here He had to say to sin on every hand, and at last suffer for sin at the cross. In the resurrection sphere He has nothing more to say to sin.

How blessed then is the vista of life — true life — that is opened to us in these verses. To live with Christ — One that loves us; to live *where* He lives — in life's eternal home; and live *as* He lives — wholly for the pleasure of God.

RECKONING OURSELVES DEAD TO SIN (6:11)
VERSE 11

The vista of blessing opened to us through the death of Christ is to have a very practical effect in the present. Faith, looking back, knows what has been accomplished on the cross (verse 6); faith, looking on, knows what the result will be in glory (verses 8-10). In the meantime, while we are yet on earth between the cross and the glory, the believer thinks of himself as dead to the principle of lawlessness. Knowing that our old man has been crucified with Christ, and that Christ has been raised from the dead and liveth to God, we are to reckon ourselves dead to sin and alive to God in Jesus Christ. We view ourselves as dead to the principle of doing our own will, which we see governs the world around, and which we find within, and we think of ourselves as living to do the will of God, as being linked up with Christ before God.

Were we actually dead there would be no need to reckon ourselves dead to sin. Were we actually in the glory there would be no need to reckon ourselves alive to God. It is just because we are still in a world that is under sin, and because we are not actually in a scene beyond the dominion of sin, that we are called upon to reckon ourselves dead to sin and alive to God.

The story of Mephibosheth has been used to set forth the believer's position in a world that has rejected Christ. Probably it is the most perfect illustration of this reckoning in scripture, for it not only makes clear the meaning of reckoning, but it also sets forth the power for the reckoning.

It will be remembered that David had shown the kindness of God to Mephibosheth for the sake of Jonathan, a picture of the grace of God that has reached us for Christ's sake (2 Samuel 9). Then, in the history of King David there came a day when he was rejected by Jerusalem (2 Samuel 15 – 18). During this time King David leaves Jerusalem and is found 'in a place that was far off' (2 Samuel 15:17). Mephibosheth, the man that had received grace from the king, is left behind in the city that had rebelled against the king. His heart, having been won by the king, has no sympathy with the scene near at hand that is in rebellion against the king. How does he act in such circumstances? 2 Samuel 19:24 tells us that 'from the day the king departed until the day he came again in peace', Mephibosheth 'had neither dressed his feet, nor trimmed his beard, nor washed his clothes'. During the time of the king's absence he acted in a way that showed that he reckoned himself dead to the scene that sur-rounded him. Stirring events were taking place in the city around him. Councils were being held, an army was being marshalled, officers were being appointed; but, in all these exciting scenes Mephibosheth takes no part. He thinks of himself as dead to it all, for he says, *All my father's house were but dead men*. Further he thinks of himself as alive to David, for he adds, 'Yet didst thou set thy servant among them that did eat at thy table'. He recognises that, as con-nected with his father's house death was upon him, but that, connected with David, he was set in life at David's table.

In the power of love for David, and in the realisation that his life is bound up with David, he acts in a way that shows he reckoned himself to be dead to the scene around him. Had he been actually dead, or had he been actually with David, there would have been no need, nor even possibility, for acting in the way he did.

Thus with the believer it is in the power of life that we are able to reckon ourselves dead to this world dominated by sin.

THE PRACTICAL RESULT OF RECKONING OURSELVES DEAD TO SIN (6:12-23)
VERSE 12

The results that follow from reckoning ourselves dead to sin are set before us in the remainder of the chapter. First, this reckoning sets us free in our practical lives from the dominion of sin. This means that the lusts connected with the mortal body are no longer obeyed.

Three things are contemplated in verse 12, the evil principle of sin, or self will, the mortal body, and the lusts of the body. Sin is the determination to do one's own will in the gratification of lust; and the body is the instrument for gratifying the lust. We are yet in these mortal bodies, and the principle of sin is still in us; but, if we reckon ourselves dead to sin and alive to God in Jesus Christ, our mortal bodies will be practically free from the dominion of sin. The *reign* of sin over these bodies is thus ended.

VERSE 13

A second result of the reckoning is that, being set free from sin, the members of the body are no longer to be yielded to sin but to God. If these different members are governed by self will it must mean that they become instruments to work unrighteousness. Being set free from the dominion of sin we are to yield *ourselves* — spirit, soul and body — and our members in particular, to God.

'Keep thy *heart* with all diligence', says the wise man; 'put away from thee a froward *mouth,* and perverse *lips* put far from thee. Let thine *eyes* look right on…. Ponder the path of thy *feet*' (Proverbs 4:23-27). What is this but the Old Testament way of expressing the New Testament exhortation 'to yield yourselves to God as alive from among the dead, and your members as instruments of righteousness to God'. We may well challenge ourselves as to what we allow in our hearts; are we imagining evil against our brother? What about our lips; do we use them to speak evil of others? What of our eyes; are they used to look upon scenes that would stir up lust and excite the flesh? What of our feet; do we allow them to carry us into places where no Christian should be found? If these, and other members, are used for such purposes they are being used for unrighteousness under the power of sin — or self will — rather than being used for righteousness and the pleasure of God.

Verse 14

A third result of reckoning ourselves dead to sin is that we come under the sustaining power of grace. This yielding ourselves and our members is not the result of being under a law that makes demands upon us, but is the outcome of being under grace that not only bring blessing to us, but sustains us and enables us to overcome. We are kept by the grace of God.

A fourth result is that we become the servants in practical righteousness (verses 15-23).

1   Reckoning ourselves dead to sin we obtain freedom from the power of sin.

2   Free from the power of sin, we can yield ourselves, and our members, to God.

3   Yielding ourselves to God we come under the sustaining grace of God.

4   Coming under the sustaining grace of God, we bring forth practical righteousness.

VERSE 15

This further truth of practical righteousness is introduced by the question, 'Shall we sin because we are not under law but under grace?' The apostle thus anticipates the reasoning of the flesh, ever ready to abuse the goodness of God and pervert the word of God. If God says, 'Where sin abounded grace did much more abound', the flesh at once says, 'Let us sin that grace may abound'. If God says, 'Ye are not under law but under grace', the flesh says — then we are set free to do what we like.

VERSE 16

The apostle entirely repudiates this carnal suggestion. He proves that the question shows entire ignorance of the terrible result of yielding to sin. 'Know ye not', says the apostle, 'that to whom ye yield yourselves servants to obey, his servants ye are to whom ye obey'. Yielding to sin, we become the slaves of sin, and every fresh indulgence of sin only forges another link in the chain that holds us in bondage to sin. An intensely solemn consideration whether for a sinner living in sin, or a saint that turns aside to trifle with sin.

Moreover, if, on the one hand, we yield to sin, or self will, it brings death in its train, or separation between the soul and God. On the other hand, if we yield ourselves by obedience to the doctrine as to death with Christ, it leads to practical righteousness.

VERSE 17

Paul could thank God that the believers at Rome, who were once the slaves of sin, had indeed obeyed from the heart the form of doctrine delivered to them. He says, not simply the doctrine, but the *form* of doctrine. This apparently was baptism, to which he has already referred in the early part of the chapter. They had believed the great truth, or doctrine, that the old man has been crucified with Christ. They had submitted to the form of the doctrine by being baptised unto the death of Christ to have part in the place of separation from sin and the world in which that death puts the believer down here. And in their daily practice they had continued to reckon themselves dead to sin and alive unto God in Christ Jesus.

With these believers it was not the mere assent of the mind to certain truths in which no personal interest was felt. It was the obedience of hearts that had learnt their need of, and personal concern in, the truths believed.

VERSE 18

Having thus obtained their freedom from sin they had become slaves to righteousness.

VERSE 19

This expression 'slaves to righteousness' might, however, be taken to imply some galling yoke with the loss of all liberty. The apostle, therefore, is careful to explain that he is simply speaking after the manner of men. Serving righteousness is not miserable slavery, but happy liberty. However, because of the infirmity of the flesh which makes it difficult for us to grasp the truth, he uses the expression 'slaves to righteousness' to contrast the happy result of being under the sway of practical righteousness, with the terrible bondage that sin has over its slaves.

To yield the members to sin is practically to become the slaves of uncleanness, and thus develop a character of lawlessness that increases in lawlessness. It leads from lawlessness to lawlessness (N.Tr.). In contrast to this, if we yield our members to the service of practical righteousness it will develop a character and condition of holiness. Here, for the first time since the introductory verses of the epistle, the apostle speaks of holiness. Yielding our members as servants to righteousness leads, not only to righteousness but also to holiness. Righteousness speaks more of outwardly right acts in relation to others; holiness refers rather to the new nature and therefore that which is inward. Thus we reach a further result of reckoning ourselves dead to sin; it leads to the development of the new nature which is holy in thought and thus separate in spirit from the world around. Not only is righteousness practised, but unrighteousness is hated.

VERSES 20-23

The apostle concludes his introduction by drawing a contrast between their past condition as slaves to sin, and their present portion as the slaves of God. When the servants of sin, they followed their own wills without any thought of the claims of righteousness. Such a course produced no lasting and pleasant fruit, but only shame and, in the end, death. It was a fruitless wasting of their lives, and the members of their bodies, in self will that covered them with shame and ended in death.

Now, having been made free from sin and become slaves to God, they brought forth the fruit of practical righteousness which leads to holiness, or that condition of heart in which evil is hated and God is known and enjoyed.

Living to God leads to the present fruit of righteousness and holiness, and the future enjoyment of eternal life in all its fullness in the glory where, not only the *power* of sin can never be felt, but the *presence* of sin can never intrude.

Here eternal life is set before us as the end of a life lived to God in this present world. But even so, it is not secured by the devotedness of the life here. It is the gift of God in

Jesus Christ our Lord. Sin pays wages: but God gives gifts. Thus the grace of God that gives the blessing is maintained; encouragement is given to live the life well pleasing to God, while the legal thought of obtaining eternal life as a reward for service is excluded.

4. DELIVERANCE FROM LAW
CHAPTER 7

In chapter six, we are instructed as to the way of deliverance from the power of sin; in chapter seven there is set before us the way of deliverance from the yoke of the law.

Obviously there is a great difference between 'sin' and 'law'. Sin came into the world by man; the law was given by God. One was absolutely evil; the other 'holy, and just, and good'. It is easy to see that we need deliverance from that which is evil; it is not so simple to learn that, as believers, we equally need to be delivered from the principle of law.

However, the consideration of the nature of the law, and its effects, should convince us of the necessity of deliverance from its dominion. First, let us remember that the law was given to the natural man to show him the standard of conduct that God requires from a man, if he is to be blessed in this world on the ground of his own doings. Secondly, in making known what God requires from man, the law also revealed the holiness and righteousness of God. Thirdly, it exposed the utter weakness and inability of man to keep the law and thus answer to God's righteous demands. Fourthly, while making demands upon man, and exposing man's weakness, it gave man no help or support to meet its requirements. Finally, the law, being holy and inflexible, utterly condemned the man that does not, in all points, keep it.

To sum up, more concisely, the principle of the law as applied to man: it makes demands upon me that I have no strength to fulfil; it gives me no strength to answer to its demands; and when I fail in carrying out its requirements, it utterly condemns me.

Thus, the law, though in itself holy and ordained to life and blessing if kept, becomes a means of showing the holiness of God, my weakness and, in consequence, my condemnation.

It becomes plain then that the believer needs deliverance from the law; and more, he needs some other support if he is to bring forth fruit to God. Verse 4 makes it very clear that it is God's desire that His people should bring forth fruit unto Himself, and thus be for His pleasure. In order that this may be so, we must know deliverance from sin, the law, and the flesh.

This brings us to the great theme of chapter seven, wherein we learn God's way of deliverance from the bondage of the law; and, that a new bond has been formed between the believer and the risen Christ in order that we may bring forth fruit to God. The chapter concludes with the experience we pass through in learning our need in order to accept God's way of deliverance.

The chapter may be divided as follows:-

First, (verses 1-3) the principle stated, and illustrated, that the law rules over a man as long as he lives.

Secondly, (verses 4-6) the application of the principle, and illustration, to the believer.

Thirdly, (verses 7-13) the use and effect of the law when applied to man in the flesh.

Fourthly, (verses 14-25) the experiences of a man who, by means of the law is learning the true nature of the flesh and his need of a deliverer.

THE ASSERTION, AND ILLUSTRATION, OF THE PRINCIPLE THAT THE DOMINION OF THE LAW ENDS WITH DEATH (7:1-3)

The great principle underlying the doctrine of chapters six and seven is that *we cannot be alive in that to which we have died.* In chapter six, this principle is applied to sin; if we have died to sin we cannot live in sin. In chapter seven this principle is applied to law; if we have died to law we are no longer under law.

VERSE 1

The apostle writes to those who 'know' the law. This would include Gentiles as well as Jews. The Jew was 'under' the law; the Gentiles, including Christendom, though not strictly under law, most certainly 'know' the law. The apostle reminds such of the well known principle 'that the law rules over a man as long as he liveth'.

This principle is illustrated by the case of the married woman. The inviolable marriage tie is used to illustrate the inviolability of the law. As long as the husband liveth the woman is bound by the law to her husband. If the husband dies she is free from the law of her husband; he has no more dominion over her. *Death has broken the bond.* She is free to be married to another. Thus the great principle is established that if God gives a law to a man a divinely formed bond is established between the law and those under it which nothing but death can annul.

THE APPLICATION TO THE BELIEVER OF THE PRINCIPLE THAT THE DOMINION OF THE LAW ENDS WITH DEATH (7:4-6)

VERSES 4-6

Having stated and illustrated the principle that death ends the rule of law, the apostle now applies this principle to believers. In the illustration the husband dies, in the application the woman dies. But this makes no difference to the principle asserted, which is that *death severs the bond*. To use the language of the illustration we die to one husband in order to be married to another. The great theme of both chapters six and seven is that we have died; but it is in Christ's death we have died. This death is set forth by the expression 'the body of Christ'. In the death of Christ we have been set free from the rule of law to come under the sway of Christ risen from the dead. Instead of our lives being controlled by a written law that is against us, we have now come under the control of a living Person that loves us.

In the illustration there are two things — *disassociation* from the first husband by death, and *association* with the second husband in life. In the application the believer is seen to be disassociated from the law by the death of Christ, and associated with the living and risen Christ. But disassociation from the law and association with Christ risen, are not simply privileges that we may enter upon, but facts true of believers *by the act of God.* God, Himself, has severed the bond with the law, for the believer, by the death of Christ — 'Ye also have been made dead to the law by the body of the Christ' (N.Tr.). We are not made dead to the law by some experience we pass through, but by the body of Christ. When the dead body of Christ hung upon the cross it was evident that He had passed out of the condition of life to which the law applied. What is true of Christ in God's sight is true of the believer in whose place Christ died.

It is thus of the first importance to see that, by the act of God Himself, we are 'not under law but under grace' (6:14).

I may practically put myself under law in a twofold way. First, by thinking that God is against me because of my sins and sin; or, secondly, by thinking God is for me on account of my fancied goodness. In either case I am making God's attitude toward me depend upon what I am for God, and that is the principle of law. Grace shows me that God is not against me because of my evil, and not for me because of my goodness; but that God is for me because of what He is in Himself, and can righteously show Himself for me because of what Christ has done.

This then is the first great truth we need to learn, that, through the death of Christ, God has set believers free from the principle of law and brought us under grace.

However, for practical deliverance from legality it is not enough to see that the old bond has been dissolved in the death of Christ, but, we must further apprehend that a new bond has been formed with Christ risen. It is as we live in the power of this new bond that our souls will be brought into liberty and we shall bring forth fruit unto God. The figure of marriage very beautifully sets forth the new bond that God has formed for the believer with Christ risen. It has been pointed out that in the marriage relationship the wife can count upon three things, the *company*, the *love* and the *support* of her husband. To be associated with the risen Christ is to have His company, enjoy His love, and obtain His support.

We see these three things very blessedly set forth when the Lord was here on earth with His disciples. They had the company, the love, and the support of Jesus. They were men of like passions with ourselves — utterly weak, often failing, ignorant and selfish. They had storms to face, privations to meet, the enemy against them; but Christ was with them, Christ loved them unto the end, and Christ supported them every step of the way.

Now He is risen, and it is our privilege still to have His company, for He has said 'I will never leave thee nor forsake thee'. We too can enjoy His love in a deeper way than it could have been known by the disciples, for it is a love that has been proved and found to be stronger than death. Moreover we have His support in a way that the disciples could hardly have realised; for it is the support of One who has triumphed over every enemy, and broken the power of death and the grave. How could we be lonely if in the company of One who is altogether lovely; how could we be dissatisfied if our hearts were filled by a love that death cannot break, time cannot change and eternity cannot end? How could we talk of our weakness if we realised that we have all the mighty power of the risen Christ to support us?

It is then in the realisation of our association with the risen Christ that we shall find practical deliverance. It is the apprehension of these two things — disassociation from the law, and association with the risen Christ — to which the soul is brought when it cries out 'I thank God through Jesus Christ our Lord'. Thus it finds deliverance from law and brings forth fruit unto God.

Verses 5-6

Furthermore it is important to see that we cannot be under the authority of the law and of Christ at the same time. The contrast between being under law and under Christ is vividly brought before us in verses 5 and 6. In verse 5 the apostle describes the effect of being under the law when we were in the flesh. He can say 'when we were in the flesh' because he is speaking from the Christian standpoint. As Christians we are no longer in the flesh, that is, the old Adam state with all its responsibilities. Looking back to that old state he describes the effect of being under the law. It excited the sinful lusts by forbidding them. Then, the passions being aroused, the members of our bodies carried them out with the result that death, or separation, came between our souls and God.

But now (in contrast to the past when we were in the flesh) all is changed; this change has been brought about by the fact that we have died with Christ. It is not that the 'law' has died, as our authorised version wrongly translates, but that we have died. It should read, 'having died in that in which we were held' (N.Tr.). The result is we no longer serve God under the sense of legal obligation — that we must do this or that in order that God may be favourable to us. That would be 'the oldness of the letter' which said 'Do this and thou shalt live'. But being set free from the principle of law we serve as in spirit delighting to do the will of God. This is the 'newness of spirit'.

THE EFFECT OF THE OPERATION OF THE LAW ON MAN IN THE FLESH (7:7-13)

VERSES 7-11

Having stated, and applied, the principle that death delivers from the bondage of the law, the apostle now shows the use of the law by describing its effect upon man in the flesh. The apostle has been pressing the truth that the believer is delivered from the law. Does, then, the necessity for this deliverance imply that the law is evil? He asks, 'Is the law sin?' The immediate answer is, 'God forbid'. The apostle then proceeds to show its use and declare its excellence.

The chief use of the law is to prove that we have in us an evil principle called 'sin'. The apostle says, 'I had not known sin, but by the law'. He does not say 'sins', but 'sin'. He would have been conscious of sins had he never known the law. We need no law to tell us it is wrong to steal and murder. Natural conscience will convict a man of wrong conduct. But conscience would never reveal to a man his inward state of sin. The law said, 'Thou shalt not lust'. This one command applies to the inward man, and, not as with the other nine commands, to the outward conduct. The outward conduct might be blameless, and consequently the conscience easy having no sense of judgement or death. But, seeing there is sin in us, the immediate effect of the law saying 'Thou shalt not lust' is to stir up lust, and at once the conscience knows that the law is broken and realises that death is the result. 'Sin revived, and I died'. The law that was ordained to life if obeyed, brings death upon the conscience when broken.

VERSES 12-13

If lust is provoked and death brought upon the conscience through the law, is the law wrong? Far from being wrong, the law is holy, and the particular commandment, 'Thou shalt not lust' is holy, and just and good.

This being so, is that which is good the cause of death? Not at all. Sin is the cause of death, not law. All the law does is to make manifest the presence and character of sin. So bad indeed is sin that it takes occasion by that which is good to bring death on the conscience. Thus the effect of the law upon a man, having lusts, is to discover to him, not only the existence of sin, but the exceeding sinfulness of sin.

THE EXPERIENCE BY WHICH THE TRUE CHARACTER OF THE FLESH IS DISCOVERED, AND THE CONSEQUENT NEED OF A DELIVERER (7:14-25)

The closing verses of the chapter give the experience of a man under law, though born again and, therefore, with renewed desires in his mind.

The experiences are presented as they appear to one who is free from the dominion of the law. Thus the apostle commences by saying, 'We know that the law is spiritual'. This 'we' represents those in the full Christian position. It is what those know who are free. Then, proceeding to give the experiences of one under law, the apostle immediately drops the 'we' and uses 'I' because the experiences set forth do not express true Christian experience. Nevertheless it is experience that, in different measures most Christians pass through.

It is deeply necessary that we should learn the true character of our old nature — the flesh, and reach the point when we have to say with Job, not only 'I am vile', but, 'I abhor myself'. We may reach this knowledge of self in three ways. First, we may learn what we are in the presence of the Lord, even as Peter when he 'fell down at Jesus' knees', and confessed, 'I am a sinful man, O Lord' (Luke 5:8). Secondly, we may learn the evil of our hearts by being trapped by the devil into some public sin, even as Peter when he denied the Lord. Lastly we may learn the character of the flesh by seeking to do what is right by our own legal efforts. It is this third way of learning ourselves that is brought before us in these experiences of the seventh of Romans. The case supposed is that of a man with renewed desires, who is seeking to do right by putting himself under the law. In all these experiences there is no mention of Christ or the Holy Spirit. The man is only thinking of the demands of the law, himself, and his own efforts.

We may be quite clear that we cannot secure salvation by keeping the ten commandments; yet, at the same time, we may be seeking to overcome the flesh, and do right, on the principle of the law. That is to say, I may be seeking to restrain the flesh by my own efforts to keep certain rules and maxims, instead of looking to Christ to support me.

The principle of law is that I secure the desired blessing by carrying out my responsibilities. I may profess that I am not under law and yet I say to myself, 'I *must not* allow this evil lust; I *must* get the victory over the old man, and indwelling sin'. In so saying I am, in principle putting myself under law; for all such thoughts simply mean that victory over sin, and deliverance from its power, depend upon my carrying out my responsibilities or, in other words, upon my own efforts. If victory over sin depends upon anything that I do, then I have wherein to boast. So slow, however, are we to accept the truth of the evil of the flesh, and our inability to overcome its evil, that these truths have to be learnt by experience, and often bitter experience. We may pass through long years of effort to overcome sin and get free from its power; but, so long as these efforts continue our history will be one of constant defeat and disappointment.

Such experiences, however useful and even necessary, will never bring about deliverance from sin. *Experience will only prove that we cannot deliver ourselves from the power of sin.* This is necessary to learn before we can be truly free; therefore while experience cannot bring about deliverance, it must, in some measure, precede deliverance.

Through these experiences, however painful, we learn some necessary lessons as the apostle shows.

VERSE 14

First, in the case supposed, the person learns that he is in *bondage under the power of sin*. He realises that the law, by which he is trying to regulate his conduct, is spiritual, but he finds that he is 'fleshly sold under sin'.

VERSE 15

He learns this experimentally, 'for', he says, 'that which I do I allow not: for what I would, that do I not; but what I hate that do I'. It is evident that if I cannot do what I would, and am driven to do what I hate, I am not a free man; I am a captive.

VERSE 16

Further, if he was doing that which he would not, it proved clearly that he consented to the law that it was good and that he was not willingly doing the evil, but was impelled by some adverse power.

VERSE 17

This power he discovers to be the evil principle of sin. So he concludes, 'It is no more I that do it, but sin that dwelleth in me'. Thus, the attempt to control and overcome the evil of his own heart by legal efforts leads to the discovery that the soul is a captive under the power of sin.

VERSE 18

Secondly, in this struggle to do right and overcome sin by legal efforts, another important truth is learnt. I discover the incorrigible evil of the flesh. As the apostle says, 'I know that in me (that is in my flesh) dwelleth no good thing'. He does not say, 'I *do* no good thing', but 'in me … dwelleth no good thing'. It is here a question of what

I am, not of what I do. As a matter of fact the flesh can do many things that are morally right. Doubtless in the case supposed, the life was blameless. The failure was lust, and that is inward.

'In the flesh' is a term used in Scripture to set forth our fallen condition, governed by the old nature, as connected with Adam. Adam innocent was in the flesh, but without sin. The Lord Jesus, too, was in the flesh, but without sin. By the fall the flesh, or nature of man, came under the dominion of sin, and so flesh became sinful flesh (Romans 8:3).

In this struggle to do right we discover that, in spite of all our efforts the flesh does not change. Lust again and again arises in the heart, showing that the old nature is there, and that it is incorrigible. We discover that not only there is a great deal of evil in the flesh, but that, in the flesh there is no good thing. We are brought to the point when we abhor ourselves.

VERSES 18-19

Thirdly, in this struggle another solemn truth is learnt — the fact that we have *no strength*. This, perhaps, is the hardest, and most humiliating truth, to learn. One has said, it is 'a great deal more humbling lesson to learn than that of the fact that certain sins have been done in the time past of my life. It raises the question, not of what I was before I knew Christ, but of what I am now that I do'.

The lesson that we have no strength in ourselves against the flesh is learnt by our vain efforts to overcome the flesh. Realising that this lust, this pride, this vanity, is wrong and must be overcome we set to work by prayer, by study of the word, and other religious exercises, to overcome these evils. In result we find that we are wearying ourselves with unavailing efforts, until at last we are compelled to say, 'How to perform that which is good I find not. For the good that I would I do not; but the evil which I would not, that I do'. Thus we learn that if victory depends upon our own efforts we must be utterly vanquished, for we have no strength. Not only is there no good thing in the flesh, but we have no strength against it. Left to ourselves and our efforts we are indeed wretched men, for our case is hopeless.

VERSES 20-23

Fourthly, in this struggle to overcome the lusts of the flesh, we learn to distinguish between ourselves and the evil principle within. 'If I do that I would not, it is no more I that do it, but sin that dwelleth in me'. There is in us a new man, which is called 'the inward man', and this new man delights in doing right. But there is also an evil principle which has power over the members of the body and wars against the desires for good that govern the inward man. In result, all these struggles to overcome the flesh by our own efforts leave us captive to the principle of sin which works in our members.

VERSE 24

Having discovered that we are chained to a body domi-nated by sin and that leads to death, we are led to look away from ourselves and cry out for a Deliverer. 'Who shall deliver me from this body of death?'

It is not simply deliverance that the soul looks for, but a Deliverer. We may indeed come to the point when we realise our need of deliverance from sin, but fail to obtain it by looking for deliverance rather than a Deliverer. The question is not, 'How shall I be delivered?' but, '*Who* shall deliver me?'

VERSE 25

At once the answer comes, 'I thank God through Jesus Christ our Lord'. The secret of deliverance is found in living 'by faith, the faith of the Son of God who loved me, and gave Himself for me'. Deliverance is not found by relying upon our prayers, our knowledge of Scripture, or our devotedness, but in looking to the Son of God. In the presence of the flesh, of the world, and of the devil — enemies that are much stronger than ourselves, we look to One who is stronger than all our enemies. The flesh is too strong for us, but the Son can make us free (John 8:36); the world is too strong for us, but the Son has overcome the world (John 16:33); Satan is too strong for us, but the Son of God was manifested to destroy the works of the devil (1 John 3:8). In looking to Him we look to One who is with us, and loves us, and can support us. We come governmentally to the truth experimentally that, in the beginning of the chapter, is stated doctrinally, the truth that we are 'married to another, even to Him that is risen from the dead, that we should bring forth fruit unto God'.

Thus deliverance is reached, but by the Deliverer. Nevertheless, this deliverance is not from the *presence* of sin, but from the *power* of sin. In heaven we shall be delivered entirely from the presence of sin. But while on earth, the flesh is still in the believer, though he is delivered from its power. The last clause of verse 25 clearly sets this forth. 'So then with the mind I myself serve the law of God; but with the flesh the law of sin'. This is a statement of the character and disposition of the new nature and the old. Deliverance from the law does not alter the disposition of the renewed mind towards the law; nor does it alter the flesh. Whether delivered or undelivered, the tendency of

the renewed mind is rightly to obey the law of God, and
of the flesh to resist God and obey sin.

5. THE BELIEVER'S POSITION IN CHRIST

CHAPTER 8

In chapter six, we learn how the believer is delivered from the power of sin, through death with Christ, that he may live to God in Christ Jesus. In chapter seven, we learn that the link with the law has been broken by Christ's death, in order that the believer may come under the support of Christ risen from the dead.

In chapter eight, there is set forth the blessings of the believer in the full Christian position, as set free from sin and the law.

The first three verses set forth the believer's position in Christ.

Verses 4-13 present the new life lived in the power of the Holy Spirit.

Verses 14-27 present the Holy Spirit, as a distinct Person, working in the believer.

Verses 28-39 present God for us in His outward operations.

THE NEW POSITION IN CHRIST (8:1-3)
VERSES 1-2

Three great truths are presented in these verses:

First, the believer's new position before God 'in Christ Jesus';

secondly, the believer's new life — the 'life in Christ Jesus';

thirdly, the new power of this life — 'the spirit of life in Christ Jesus'.

We learn that God has set the believer before His face in an entirely new position 'in Christ Jesus', in contrast to our old position before God as unbelievers, 'in Adam'. In 1 Corinthians 15:22, we have the two expressions used in contrast. There we read, 'As *in Adam* all die, even so *in Christ* shall all be made alive'. To be in Adam is to be before God in the same position as Adam fallen; that is, to be under God's displeasure as having disobeyed God, to be under judgement on account of sin, and to be rejected or driven from the presence of God. To be in Christ is to be before God in the same position in which Christ risen is in; that is to be in the favour of God, free from judgement and accepted.

It is thus the believer's privilege to look at Christ, and say: 'My position before God is set forth in Christ risen, and at the right hand of God. He is in the everlasting favour of God, and I am in the same favour (Romans 5:2). He has been into my judgement and is for ever beyond judgement, and 'there is therefore now no condemnation' for me. He has been received into the glory, and I am accepted in Him — the Beloved' (Ephesians 1:6).

Secondly, not only, as believers, are we in a new position before God, but we have also a new life in Christ Jesus. As

111

we can learn the blessedness of the new position by contrasting it with the old, so we are helped to appreciate the blessedness of this new life in Christ, by contrasting it with the old life in Adam. The old life lived in Adam is a life dominated by sin, which means it is a life lived in self will, without reference to God; it is a life under the condemnation of God, and a life that ends in death. The life in Christ is a new life which has Christ for its object, over which sin has no power, to which no condemnation attaches, and which death cannot end. It is a life that has had its perfect expression in Christ, so that believers can say, 'Christ is our life' (Colossians 3:4).

Thirdly, the believer is not only set before God in a new position, with a new life, but a new power — the Holy Spirit — is given to the believer to enable him to enter into the blessedness of the new position and live the new life. This life, lived in the power of the Spirit, will be the reproduction of the beautiful life of Christ, manifesting itself in 'love, joy, peace, longsuffering, kindness, goodness, fidelity, meekness, self-control' (Galatians 5:22, N.Tr.).

There is a great difference between possessing life and living the life we possess. God has imparted to us, not only the life of the risen Christ, but He has given us the Holy Spirit to enable us to live and enjoy the life. It is of the deepest importance to see that a Divine Person has come to dwell in the believer connected with the new life. The Holy Spirit has nothing to say to the flesh, or the old life, except to condemn and set it aside.

Moreover, the Spirit always acts according to one unchanging principle, for this is the meaning of the expression 'the law of the Spirit'. Law is an unchanging unbending principle. Thus the law of the Spirit is always to set aside in the believer that which has been con-demned and set aside in the death of Christ, in order to manifest in the believer the life of the risen Christ. By the action of the Spirit, engaging our hearts with Christ, we are practically set free from the law of sin and death.

It is well to remark that this freedom is not said to be from the presence of sin and death, but from the '*the law* of sin and death'. While down here we shall not be free from the presence of sin, but, by 'the law of the Spirit of life in Christ Jesus' we are made free from the *power* of sin and death.

VERSE 3

Furthermore, God cannot impart the new life without dealing with the old life. If the old man is under the judgement of God, that judgement must be executed. Therefore we read, 'God having sent His own Son, in like-ness of flesh of sin, and for sin, has condemned sin in the flesh' (N.Tr.).

If we have learnt the utter vileness of our own hearts, and that in consequence we are under condemnation and death, we cannot rest until we see that all this evil has been dealt with by God, to God's satisfaction, and that the judgement and death that was upon us has been borne.

What a relief to learn that God, Himself, has dealt with our sinful state as children of Adam, and all its conse-quences. It is God that has undertaken our case. God has not overlooked or ignored our sinful state. On the con-trary, by sending His own Son in the likeness of sinful flesh, and as a sacrifice for sin, He has at the cross con-demned sin in the flesh. When made a sacrifice for sin, all our sinful state came up before God in the Person of our Representative or Substitute. As such, all God's holy judgement against sin fell upon Him. Had it fallen upon us we should have been lost for ever; but it fell upon One who, by reason of the greatness of His Person 'His own Son' — could exhaust the judgement. When the judgement fell upon Christ, God saw our judgement being endured. When He died, in God's sight we died, as we read, 'Our old man is crucified with Him'.

Thus we learn that what the law could not do, has been accomplished at the cross. The law could condemn the sinner but could not remove the condemnation.

THE NEW LIFE LIVED IN THE POWER OF THE SPIRIT (8:4-13)

In this portion of the chapter we have unfolded to us the practical results that follow from this new life lived in the power of the Holy Spirit.

VERSE 4

First, if we walk according to the Spirit, *the practical requirements of the law are fulfilled.* One has said ' The law is not the measure of Christian walk; it only says that he who walks according to the Spirit fulfils it....The Spirit will assuredly not lead us into that which is contrary to the law of God. The law is practically fulfilled, while we are not under the law, but under the guidance of the Spirit' (J.N.Darby). The requirements of the law are fulfilled, not by making the law a rule of life, but by walking in this new life according to the Spirit.

VERSE 5

Secondly, if we walk according to the Spirit *we shall mind the things of the Spirit.* This will take us a great way beyond fulfilling the requirements of the law. The law does not go beyond regulating our conduct on earth in the varied relationships of life. The 'things of the Spirit' are heavenly things in connection with the heavenly relationships that belong to the life in Christ Jesus.

They that walk according to the desires of the flesh will have their minds set on the things of this world that the flesh can alone appreciate. The Spirit has nothing to say to the things of this world apart from the interests of Christ. We may well challenge our hearts with the question, 'Are our minds set on the things of the flesh or the things of the Spirit?'

VERSE 6

Thirdly, *a walk according to the Spirit will lead to life and peace.* The Spirit leads the soul into the enjoyment of life, and thus keeps the soul in calm peace, amidst all the turmoil and confusion of this world. He is indeed the power of that fountain of life within, that springs up unto everlasting life. To follow the mind of the flesh is to bring the sense of death upon the soul, by putting it out of touch with God. Another has said, 'All the workings of the desire and will of the flesh end in death. Yea have the principle of death in them, for it is living without God' (J.N.Darby). So we read, in 1 Timothy 5:6, 'She that liveth in pleasure (or 'in habits of self indulgence') *is dead while she liveth*'. Death is separation from God. Minding the things of the flesh will, not only hinder our communion, but will bring in the sense of separation from God in the soul of the believer.

VERSES 7-8

This must be so seeing the flesh is entirely contrary to God. It is enmity to God. It loves the things that God hates; and hates the things that God loves. Moreover, it rebels against the authority of God. 'It is not subject to the law of God neither indeed can be'. It follows, therefore, that 'they that are in the flesh' — that stand before God in the position of Adam — 'cannot please God'. It does not say that such cannot please man, or do a great many things that are kind and beneficial to the world. Besides doing evil, the flesh can do things that are morally good; but in all these things, self, in some form, is the motive. Therefore, whatever else the flesh can do, it cannot please God.

Verse 9

Fourthly, having the Spirit, in connection with this new life, *the believer is viewed as in a new condition, 'in the Spirit'.* In the beginning of the chapter the believer is looked at as in a new position — 'in Christ', in contrast to the old position, in Adam. Here he is viewed as in a new condition, 'in the Spirit' in contrast with the old condition, 'in the flesh'.

This condition is another consequence of having the Holy Spirit, for the apostle says, 'Ye are … in the Spirit, if so be that the Spirit of God dwell in you'.

Here man's natural condition is set in contrast with the full Christian condition. No intermediate condition is taken into account. It is not a contrast between the natural man and a man born again, but rather the contrast between the natural man and what is true of a Christian — one who is indwelt by the Holy Spirit. The Old Testament saints were born again by the Spirit as truly as the New Testament saints, but such are not contemplated in this passage.

The part of the verse that states that 'if any man have not the Spirit of Christ he is none of His', is parenthetical. You are either a Christian with the Spirit and of Christ, or a natural man without the Spirit and not of Christ.

These are the two conditions recognised in the verse. There may indeed by a state short of the full Christian condition in a soul born of God, but not yet brought to believe in Christ risen and exalted at God's right hand, but such a condition is not alluded to in the verse. It would be wrong to deduce from this verse that the Old Testament saints must have had the Spirit indwelling them as otherwise they could not be Christ's.

VERSE 10

Fifthly, another blessed result of having the Spirit is that Christ can be said to be 'in us'. Not only is the believer in Christ before God, but *Christ is in the believer characteristically before men.*

The Holy Spirit is spoken of as the Spirit of Christ, because it was in the power of the Spirit that Christ acted in His life (Acts 10:38); offered Himself up to God in death (Hebrews 9:14), and by whom He was raised from the dead. It has been said that 'His whole life was the expression of the operation of the Spirit — of the Spirit in man'.

If the Spirit that acted in Christ so perfectly, dwells in the believer it must be in order to express or reproduce the character of Christ in the believer, so that it can be said Christ is in us. But if Christ be in us by the Spirit, then the Spirit must be the energy of this spiritual life in order that there may be practical righteousness. If the flesh is the energy of life it can only be to bring forth sin, and the body is the instrument by which the flesh expresses itself. Therefore the body is held to be dead *so far as sin is concerned*, but the Spirit, who now dwells in the body, is the source and energy of life in view of practical righteousness.

VERSE 11

Sixthly, there is yet another great operation of the Holy Spirit — *the final deliverance of our mortal bodies from the*

117

presence of sin and death. The Holy Spirit is the Spirit of God who raised up Jesus from the dead. If the Spirit of God dwells in us, God will accomplish in us what He has already accomplished in Christ.

We have then, in the opening verses of this chapter, verses 1-11, the truth of what God has wrought in the past for the believer, what God is doing in the present with the believer, and what God will yet do in the future for the complete deliverance of His people. In the past He has, through the sacrifice of the Lord Jesus at the cross, condemned sin in the flesh; in the present He sets us free from the law of sin and death through the Spirit of life in Christ Jesus; and in the future, the power of God, acting through His Spirit, will accomplish the perfect and final deliverance of the body itself.

VERSES 12-13

The practical conclusion for the believer is that he owes nothing to the flesh. The flesh, viewed as an evil principle, has no longer any rights over us. Living after the flesh only ends in death; but if, by the Spirit, we mortify the deeds of the body we shall live. The deeds of the body are all those things which are the result of the flesh working through the body.

The apostle says, 'we are debtors not to the flesh', but he does not say we are debtors to the Spirit, because this would be putting us under a higher law, the fulfilment of which would be more impossible than the Mosaic law. It is not that we are not responsible to live after the Spirit, but that this responsibility is not carried out by legal obligation but by the power of the new affections which the Spirit imparts.

It is important to see that while we have a new life with spiritual faculties capable of enjoying God, yet this life is a dependent life that needs power and must have an object. In Romans seven we see a man with the new life 'delighting in the law of God after the inward man', but with neither power nor object. In these opening verses of chapter 8, there is the new life with Christ the Object for which to live, and the Spirit the power by which to live.

THE HOLY SPIRIT, AS A DISTINCT PERSON, WORKING IN THE BELIEVER (8:14-27)

In the first thirteen verses, the Spirit, though spoken of as indwelling the believer, is viewed more especially in connection with the new life. The truth presented is rather what God works *with us* as identified with the new life. In this second portion of the chapter, verses 14-27, the Spirit is viewed as a distinct Person working *in us*. In the latter part of the chapter, verses 28-39, it is not so much God with us, or in us, but God working *for us* in His outward operations.

VERSE 14

The first great effect of being led by the Spirit of God is to produce in believers the character that is proper to the sons of God, so that characteristically such are sons of God.

VERSES 15-16

Moreover such will not only be characteristically sons, but consciously sons. They will cry 'Abba Father'. This, as one has said, 'is a distinct definite testimony of the Spirit who dwells in us that we are children; not a proving by the word' (J.N.Darby). We are thus brought into the position of sons, and the relationship of children.

VERSES 17-18

Moreover, if we are children we are heirs. An heir is one who has an inheritance in prospect. Further, if believers

119

are the heirs of God, they are joint heirs with Christ, and therefore, our inheritance is nothing less than glory with Christ. How blessed then is our prospect. Did we but realise the blessedness and reality of these great truths, how differently we should think of one another. Poor and ignorant we may be, and of little account in the eyes of this world; but, in the light of our glorious inheritance, the highest honours that this world can confer are of small account. It doth not yet appear what we shall be.

In the meantime we are called to 'suffer with Him'. Other Scriptures speak of suffering *for Him* on account of our testimony. Here it is the common lot of all believers to suffer *with Him,* implying that we feel with Him the sorrows of the world that we are passing through. When here He felt in His spirit the sorrow and the pain, the hunger and the want, the sickness and the distress that sin had brought into the world. He was touched with compassion, He sighed deeply because of the hardness of men; and He wept over sinners. If led by the Spirit we shall feel, in our little measure, even as He felt, not merely with human sympathy but with Divine compassion.

We are passing through a world from which Christ has been rejected — a world of vanity, sin and sorrow. The effect of knowing God as our Father, and the blessedness of the scene of glory to which we are going, only gives us a deeper sense of the sorrows and miseries of the world we are passing through. But the sufferings of this present time are not worthy to be compared with the glories that are coming. The sufferings are passing, the glories are eternal.

Verses 19-21

The creature is in the state of misery and corruption which results from the fall, and will be so until the sons of

God are manifested in bodies of glory. With the creatures it is no question of souls that need to be redeemed, but of bodies that are subject to corruption. The sons are the subjects of grace that has redeemed their souls and given them an inheritance in glory. The creature cannot be the subject of grace, but will share in the glory that will bring the outward blessing to this world of sorrow. For this deliverance from corruption the creature waits for the manifestation of the glory of the sons of God.

It was not by the will of the creature that it became subject to vanity, but through the folly of man. But the glory is coming, therefore, if the creature is subject to vanity, it is so in hope of deliverance from the bondage of corruption. If it cannot share in the liberty of grace that sets free from sin and judgement, it will share in the liberty of glory that lifts every pressure from these bodies.

Verse 22

Thus the Christian is not in ignorance of the misery of the groaning creation. Led by the Spirit, believers have the mind of Christ and can say '*We know* that the whole creation groaneth and travaileth in pain together until now'. Those who reject the fall impute all the misery of a groaning creation to natural causes, and, in their folly, imagine they can remove the misery by their own efforts. We know that from the fall until now the creation groans and travails in pain, and will do so, until the manifestation of the sons of God.

Verse 23

Moreover, not only do we know the true character of the groaning creation, but we can sympathise with the creature's groan. Having divine intelligence through the Spirit, and the divine affections of the new life, on the one hand, and a body that links us up with a fallen creation on the other, we are able to enter into the sorrows and miseries of a groaning creation. Groaning is feeling the misery according to God. Our sense of sorrow springs from more than being mere onlookers, for we are united to a groaning creation by bodies which are subject to vanity, sickness, pain, and death.

This groaning, however, is not a complaint, the fruit of discontent, but the operation of the Holy Spirit in the heart. God permits a groan, but never a grumble. In the meantime we wait for the adoption — the full blessing, when the body will be redeemed.

VERSE 24

The redemption of the body is a matter of hope, and in this sense we are 'saved in hope'. The hope does not imply any uncertainty, but only that the blessing is not yet manifested. 'Hope that is seen is not hope; for what a man seeth, why doeth he yet hope for?'

VERSE 25

With this hope shining before us, we can with patience wait the certainty of the glory which in due time will be revealed. If we view the sorrows around us in a selfish spirit, or as mere moralising onlookers, we shall grow weary and impatient, because of the power of evil. If we view it all in the power of the Spirit we shall 'with patience wait'.

To sum up the truth of these verses: *we know* the true character of this scene, *we groan* in divine sympathy with its misery, *we wait* for the redemption of the body, we wait *in hope*, and we wait *in patience*.

VERSES 26-27

As we survey the accumulating sorrows of this groaning creation, and realise our need, we may indeed find relief in prayer; but, even so, we know not how to pray as we ought. However much we may know of Christ, or of ourselves, or of the sorrows of the groaning creation around, it will ever be true that, while down here, we shall only know in part. We are not competent to take in the greatness and glory of Christ, or the weakness and infirmities of the flesh, and the sorrows of the groaning creation. But One has come to dwell in us Who, on the one hand, is competent to make known the love of God and take of the things of Christ and show them unto us; and, on the other hand, knows all the depth of our need and is able to present that need to God. The Holy Spirit can present the glories of Christ to us, and present our need and weakness to God.

Moreover, moved by the Spirit of God our needs are presented with an earnestness that no human words can express. A groan always presumes a depth of feeling beyond the power of words to utter. For this reason, only God can interpret a groan. Therefore it is said, 'He that searcheth the hearts knoweth what is the mind of the Spirit', even though the mind of the Spirit is expressed in us by a groan.

Furthermore, being a Divine Person, the Spirit maketh intercession for the saints according to the will of God. There may be much weakness and defect in our intercessions. We may intercede for one another according to what we think will be best for one another, or according to the course we should like the answer to take, and therefore our requests may often fall short of 'the will of God'.

If our infirmities prevent us knowing how to pray as we ought, the Spirit comes to our help. First, He makes intercession for us; secondly, He intercedes with groanings; thirdly, He intercedes according to the will of God.

Christ, the Minister of the Sanctuary, intercedes in heaven to keep us in accord with the glory of that scene. The Holy Spirit, dwelling in the saints on earth, intercedes according to the perfect knowledge of our wilderness needs.

GOD FOR US IN HIS OUTWARD OPERATIONS (8:28-30)
VERSE 28

The apostle has shown how blessedly the Holy Spirit works in us by the new life in Christ, and the indwelling Holy Spirit, producing spiritual experiences. Now we learn that not only is God the Holy Spirit in us, but that God is *for us* in 'all things' that are taking place around us. In regard to all the circumstances of life, the trials, the sorrows, the conflicts and the difficulties, we may not know how to pray as we ought; but this we do know, 'That all things work together for good to them that love God'. We may not always see how this loss, or that trial, is working for our good, but faith knows that good will be the result in time and eternity. To understand the way in which all things work for good we may have to wait, even as the Lord said to Peter, 'What I do thou knowest not now; but thou shalt know hereafter'. Another has said, 'The sorrow may not be remedied, but the sorrow is blessed'.

To assure our hearts that all is working for good, we are reminded that we are 'the called' of God; and, if called, God has a purpose for us. God saves us because we need saving; God calls us because He wants us. All God's ways with us in the present have in view the fulfilment of His purpose for us in the future.

124

VERSE 29

We are left in no doubt as to the blessedness of God's purpose for us. This purpose centres in His Son. God has purposed to have a vast host conformed to the image of His Son, and that this great company be in relationship with Christ as His brethren, amongst whom Christ will be supreme — the Firstborn.

Calling presumes God's foreknowledge. None can deny such foreknowledge to God; but if He foreknows it is equally easy for God to predestinate our future. Predestination would always appear to have in view some special and distinguishing blessing to which we are called. Moreover, in view of the predestined blessing, we have been justified. Justification has in view the glory. We are not justified in order to be exalted in this world, but to be glorified with Christ in the world to come. Nevertheless, though we wait for the glory, it is, like justification, referred to as if already accomplished. Is not this because all is here presented as from God's side, and God can call that which is not as if it were. We have the flesh in us; we have a body subject to infirmity and weakness; we are surrounded by a groaning creation; we have to meet trials and difficulties, sorrow and suffering; but faith realises that God is for us. Before the groaning creation God was for us; in, and through it all, God is for us; above it all, God is for us, and beyond it all, God is for us. In this great passage it is not what we may be for God, but what God is for us, and the marvellous fact that the very sin by which we have ruined ourselves has become the occasion for God showing Himself to be for us.

VERSES 31-32

The conclusion is that 'if God be for us who can be against us?' Unbelief may look at the trials and sorrows and difficulties of the way, and the question may arise in the soul, 'Can God be for me after all?' Faith knows that the everlasting witness that God is for us is not found in the circumstances that we pass through, but in the gift of the Son. If God 'spared not His own Son, but delivered Him up for us all', He must indeed be 'for us'. If He has already given the greatest gift we need have no question as to the blessings He has given and purposed for us. Having spared not His Son at the cross, but delivered Him up for us all, He can now righteously and freely give us 'all things'.

Verse 33

Arising out of the great truth that God is for us, there is a threefold challenge. First, 'Who shall lay anything to the charge of God's elect?' The simple and blessed answer that meets every charge is, 'it is God that justifieth'.

Verse 34

Secondly, 'who is he that condemneth?' If God justifies, who can condemn? To answer this question the apostle brings together in one verse, the death, resurrection and ascension of Christ. Already the epistle has shown that God justifies the believer through the death of Christ, and sets forth the perfection of this justification in the resurrection of Christ. Now in the glory He intercedes on behalf of those whom He has justified. If there is an active enemy ever ready to accuse the saints, there is a living Person who intercedes on their behalf.

Verse 35

This leads to the third challenge, 'Who shall separate us from the love of Christ?' The apostle enumerates seven forms of trial. Every form of evil that we have to meet in passing through this world can be ranged under one or

CHRIST THE HEAD OF A NEW RACE

other of these trials. In varied measures and at different times we may have to face some of these trials, but not one of these things can separate us from the love of Christ.

Verses 36-37

The word is quoted to show that the saints of old were exposed to these trials, and often in such extreme form that it could be said all day long they were in danger of death, and were thus looked upon by the world as sheep for the slaughter. But this did not separate them from the love of Christ. They were more than conquerors; they not only stood fast in the trial, but they were blessed in the trial, 'through Him that loved us'.

Verses 38-39

The apostle has spoken of the visible dangers of the present life and of the love of Christ. He closes by referring to invisible dangers, and the love of God. He enumerates a list of the far deeper difficulties than those connected with the temporal life. He speaks of death with its terrors, and life with its mysteries, and of the invisible and spiritual powers than can be ranged against us, and of things to come as well as things present. We are conscious of our insufficiency to meet the temporal dangers to which we are exposed. How much greater our helplessness in the presence of invisible and spiritual powers. Nevertheless, says the apostle, for our comfort, 'I am persuaded' that none of these things 'shall be able to separate us from the love of God' — that love which has found its perfect expression 'in Christ Jesus our Lord'.

DIVISION 3

GOD'S DISPENSATIONAL DEALINGS

Chapters 9 – 11

1.   INTRODUCTORY

In the first part of the epistle, all mankind, whether Jews or Gentiles, have been convicted by the word of God, of being on one common level as sinners under judgement before God, and without strength to save themselves from the judgement.

Then there is unfolded to us the way in which God has wrought in righteousness in the blessing of man through the death and resurrection of the Lord Jesus. The blessing thus secured, for those who believe, is fully summed up in chapter 8.

At once, however, a difficulty arises in the mind of the Jew. This sovereign grace that concludes all alike under judgement, and holds out blessing for all, might appear to set aside the special promises made to Israel. It is clear from Genesis chapters 15, 17 and 18 that God had purposes of blessing for, and through, Israel. These purposes of blessing for Israel and the world, were set forth in the unconditional promises made to Abraham. The question then arises, how is it possible to reconcile the sovereign grace of God to all with the special promises made to the fathers in favour of Israel? This difficulty is met in the third division of the epistle — chapters nine, ten and eleven. These chapters unfold to us the ways of God with Israel and the world during successive periods, or dispensations in the history of the world. They set forth the perfect consistency of God's sovereign grace with His special promises to Israel.

Chapter nine proves that the sovereign grace of God is the alone ground of all blessings whether for Israel or the Gentile.

Chapter ten shows that the fall of Israel opens the way for sovereign grace to bless the Gentile.

Chapter eleven foretells that the rejection of the grace of God by the Gentile will prepare the way for the restoration of Israel.

2. GRACE THE ONLY GROUND OF BLESSING FOR ALL

CHAPTER 9

The Jews not only objected to the doctrines of grace taught by the apostle, but they opposed the apostle himself. They said that the apostle taught all men everywhere against the people, the law and the temple (Acts 21:28).

In chapter nine, the apostle replies to these objections. First, he takes up the personal question in verses 1-5. Then, in the remainder of the chapter, he meets the objection that the grace of God to all makes void the special promises to Israel. He clearly proves that while every promise will be fulfilled it will be on the ground of grace.

VERSES 1-5

As to himself, so far from being against his kinsmen according to the flesh, he has great heaviness and continual sorrow on their behalf. Indeed, the wish had passed through his mind, that he, himself, might be accursed from Christ, if it were possible by this means to bring blessing to Israel. Moreover, how could he think lightly of those to whom pertain the adoption, the glory, the covenants, the giving of the law, the services, the promises, and above all, of whom, as concerning the flesh, Christ came, Who is over all, God blessed forever.

It was not Paul who made light of Israel's privileges, but rather the accusers of Paul, for had they not rejected their Messiah? As he says in the end of the chapter 'they stumbled at that stumblingstone', rejecting Christ as being merely a carpenter. Paul, on the contrary, maintained His glory, asserting He is God over all blessed forever.

VERSE 6

Having answered the attacks on himself, the apostle passes on to prove that the sovereign grace of God taking up the Gentile, does not make the word of God, that gave special promises to Israel, of none effect.

Paul had been teaching that all, whether Jew or Gentile, came into blessing on the ground of sovereign grace. At once the Jew raises the objection that this teaching denies the promises which came to them on the ground of *natural descent*. To this objection the apostle replies that not all those who are of Israel by natural descent are the true Israel of God to whom the promises were made. He then turns to Scripture to prove his contention.

VERSES 7-9

He appeals first to the history of Abraham. Here, clearly, if the Jew insists upon natural descent he must admit the Arabians into blessing, for they were descended from Abraham through Ishmael (Genesis 25:12-18). Natural descent is then shut out. With Isaac we see the blessing secured on the principle of sovereign electing grace, for the word is, 'In Isaac shall a seed be called to thee'. Ishmael was the child of flesh, but Isaac was the child of promise. That this promise was according to sovereign grace is made abundantly plain by the word, 'At this time *will I come* and Sarah shall bare a son'.

VERSES 10-12

The apostle next takes up the story of Isaac and proves the same principle by his two sons. In regard to Abraham, a Jew might object that the sons were by different mothers; but no such objection could be raised in the case of the sons of Isaac. Jacob and Esau were both the sons of Rebecca. If then the blessing is by *natural descent* the seed of both sons would inherit the promises; but then the Jew would have to include the Edomite. This no Jew would do. Here again, then, natural descent is shut out, and the blessing is seen to be on the ground of sovereign choice, which said, 'The elder shall serve the younger'. Moreover this was said before they were born, and therefore before they had 'done any good or evil' proving that God's sovereign call does not depend upon the works of the one that is called, but upon the grace of the One that calls.

VERSE 13

Furthermore, long centuries after their lives had been lived, and their characters had been developed, God had said 'Jacob have I loved, but Esau have I hated'. Jacob, with all his many faults, was a man of faith, and comes into blessing on the ground of grace. Esau, with many natural excellencies, had no fear of God, and misses the blessing though the elder son by natural descent.

VERSES 14-15

To these arguments the flesh may object, that to elect one and not the other is unrighteous. Is there, then, unrighteousness with God? God forbid, says the apostle. To answer this objection the apostle refers to a specific case in the history of Israel in which it is plain that God acted in

sovereign grace and yet could not be charged with
unrighteousness. He recalls the terrible sin of Israel when
they made a golden calf and worshipped it. Of the
unrighteousness of this act there can be no question. They
had broken the first command, and the penalty was death.
Righteousness could have destroyed them all. But what
did God do? He fell back on His sovereignty and said, 'I
will have mercy upon whom I will have mercy, and I will
have compassion on whom I will have compassion'. God
falls back upon the very principle to which the Jew
objects, and but for which all Israel would have been
destroyed. It is impossible, then, for the Jew to say it was
unrighteous of God to act in sovereign grace.

VERSE 16

Thus the apostle shows that blessing is no question of
man's will, or man's activities, but is entirely dependent
upon the sovereign grace of God which showeth mercy.

VERSES 17-18

A further objection might, however, be raised. Some
might say, 'We can see there was no unrighteousness in
the case of Israel and the calf, when God used His sovereignty to bless; but how about the case when God acts in
judgement?' To answer this objection, the apostle takes
the case of Pharaoh to show that God is not unrighteous
in judgement.

In setting up the golden calf, Israel did wickedly, and God
in sovereignty showed mercy. Pharaoh also did wickedly,
and God judged him. Where does the sovereignty of God
come in here? Is it not seen in the fact that, again and
again, God acted in sovereign mercy in removing the
plagues. But this mercy only became the occasion of
Pharaoh hardening his heart (see Exodus 7:13, 22; 8:15,
19, 32; 9:7, N.Tr.). Finally, Pharaoh having hardened his

heart, we read that, 'The LORD hardened the heart of Pharaoh' (Exodus 9:12).

God did not make Pharaoh wicked. God leads no man to sin; but when Pharaoh had proved himself wicked and stubborn, God judicially hardened his heart. This hardening, however, never takes place until man has proved himself to be wicked. The natural fallen man as described in Romans one, first gives up God before he is given up by God. So with Israel, the nation heard 'the report of the Lord' and had seen 'the arm of the Lord', and rejected both His words and works, before the word is applied to them, 'He hath blinded their eyes and hardened their hearts' (John 12:37-41).

So will it be with Christendom, 'Because they received not the love of the truth, that they might be saved, and for *this cause* God shall send them strong delusion, that they should believe a lie' (2 Thessalonians 2:10).

It is therefore true that, whether acting in sovereign mercy or in judgement, God acts according to His will. 'Therefore hath He mercy on whom *He will* have mercy, and whom *He will* He hardeneth'; and in either case He acts righteously.

VERSES 19-21

But someone will say: If this is so, 'Why doth He yet find fault?' Who hath resisted His will? If God hardens a man, how can the man help himself, and how can God find fault with the man? The apostle's first answer to this objection is a very peremptory one. He asks, 'Who are you to find fault with God?' Supposing you do not understand, is God to give an account of His matters to you? We have to remember that we are mere men and that God is God, and we do well to give Him His place as God. God is the One that forms. Man is the thing formed, and shall the thing formed complain to the One that forms, 'Why hast Thou made me thus?' Has not the potter absolute power over the clay — to make one vessel unto honour, or, if he so wills, to make a vessel unto dishonour? The apostle thus establishes the absolute right of God to act as He will, without giving account of His matters to man. Nevertheless, while the illustration of the potter asserts in the strongest way the absolute right of God to do as He pleases, it does not teach that God *has made any vessel to dishonour*. The illustration simply asserts and maintains God's prerogatives.

VERSES 22-23

The way God *uses* this absolute power is seen in His actings towards the vessels of wrath and the vessels of mercy. As regards the vessels of wrath, it truly says, 'they are fitted for destruction', but it does not say that God fitted them for destruction. He made His power known, not by fitting them for destruction, but, by enduring them with much longsuffering. As regards the vessels of mercy, it does say of such, He 'had afore prepared unto glory'. God endured the Amorites of old with much longsuffering until they fitted themselves for destruction by their iniquities being come to the 'full'. Then the judgement fell. (Genesis 15:16).

VERSE 24

The vessels of mercy are seen in those called by the gospel in sovereign grace, not of the Jews only but also of the Gentiles. Once allow that all blessing rests upon the sovereignty of God, the Gentile must be admitted to the blessing as well as the Jew.

VERSES 25-26

The apostle proves his argument by turning to the Jews' own Scriptures. In verse 25 he quotes from Hosea 2:23 to prove the call of the Jew: then, in verse 26, he quotes from Hosea 1:10, to prove the call of the Gentile.

VERSES 27-29

Further, the apostle quotes the prophet Isaiah to show that, numerous as the people of Israel were, only a remnant would be saved. That this remnant was spared was entirely owing to the sovereign grace of the Lord, as the prophet says, 'Except the Lord of Sabaoth had left us a seed, we had been as Sodom, and had been like unto Gomorrha'. But for grace they would have been totalled destroyed.

VERSES 30-33

The apostle sums up his argument by showing that the Gentiles have obtained the blessing on the principle of faith while Israel has missed the blessing by seeking it on the principle of law. Trusting in their own righteousness they refused grace and rejected the One who came in lowly grace. They stumbled at the stumblingstone — Christ in humility.

3. GRACE BLESSING THE GENTILE ON THE FALL OF ISRAEL

CHAPTER 10

The teaching of chapter 9 proves, not only that God's dealing in sovereign grace to all is perfectly consistent with His special promises to Israel, but, that the promises to Israel can only be fulfilled on the principle of grace.

The tenth chapter shows that Israel, having been tested by the gospel of God's sovereign grace, has stumbled and fallen; and that the fall of Israel has opened the door of blessing to the Gentile.

VERSES 1-2

The apostle opens this part of his epistle by again asserting his love for Israel. His heart's desire and prayer to God was that Israel might be saved. He can bear them witness that they have a zeal for God, though not according to knowledge of God as revealed in Christ through the gospel.

VERSES 3-4

The apostle then shows how Israel has missed the blessing. Being ignorant of the righteousness of God revealed in the gospel, they went about seeking to establish their own righteousness according to the law. Clinging to their own righteousness they did not submit to the righteousness of God. The gospel clearly shows that Christ is the end of the law for righteousness, to every one that believes. Alas, Israel had not believed in Christ. They had stumbled at Christ.

VERSES 6-8

The apostle then contrasts the righteousness which is of the law, and the righteousness which is of faith. Strangely enough, as we might think, he finds a proof that the blessing is secured by faith in the writings of Moses. The principle of the law is plainly 'that the man which doeth' the things commanded by the law shall live by so doing. If he keeps the law he will obtain life by his own righteousness. The believer, however, realises that he has not kept, and cannot keep, the law, and having failed to do right cannot secure the blessing on that ground. Then follows a remarkable quotation from Deuteronomy to show the way faith takes.

In this passage, Deuteronomy 30:11-14, Moses looks on to the time when Israel has utterly failed on the ground of their own doings, and has been driven out of the land and scattered 'among all nations'. Then, in their misery, if they turn to the Lord with all their heart, they will take up the language of faith. When all is over on the ground of law, they will turn to God in simple faith.

Faith does not say, 'Who shall ascend into heaven?' We have not to ascend to heaven to ask God to come to our help; that would be a denial that Christ has come from heaven. Nor does faith say, 'Who shall descend into the deep?' That would be a denial that Christ has been into death and is risen from the dead. Israel, clinging to their own works, ignored the mighty facts of the gospel — that

141

Christ had come, had been into death, and was risen from the dead.

What then does faith say? Faith realises that the blessing cannot be obtained by our works, but only through Christ and hence to receive a blessing is a question of the con- fession of Christ with the mouth as the outcome of faith in the heart. The word is nigh thee *in thy mouth* and *in thy heart.*

Verses 9-10

Applying the principle of the quotation, the apostle shows that our blessing is secured through faith in Christ, the reality of which is proved by the confession of the lips. Christ is presented to the soul as the One who has done a work to meet the glory of God, and the need of man. The needy soul believes the glad tidings in his heart. To believe in the heart is to believe as having a personal interest in that which is believed. I believe as seeing the personal importance of what Christ has done for myself. I see that I need Christ and His work for my salvation, and that without Christ I am lost forever. As one has said 'The faith of the heart produces the confession of the mouth: thus the confession of the mouth becomes the proof of the sincerity of the faith'.

Verse 11

Furthermore, the one confessing the Name of Jesus, will find that he has the support of God in answer to that Name, as Isaiah says, 'Whosoever believeth in Him will not be ashamed' (Isaiah 28:16). God will not allow the one that confesses the Name of Christ to be confounded (See Acts 4:9-22).

VERSES *12-13*

If then the blessing is free to 'whosoever believeth', as the quotation from Isaiah proves, it must be for the Gentile as well as the Jew. Already the apostle has shown that there is 'no difference' on our side — all are under sin before God (Romans 3:22-23); now he shows there is 'no difference' on God's side. God is acting in grace towards all, is rich unto all that call upon Him. With this the Jewish Scriptures agree, for Joel says, 'Whosoever shall call on the name of the Lord shall be saved' (Joel 2:32).

VERSES *14-15*

But before people can call upon the Lord they must of necessity hear about the Lord, and this calls for a preacher sent from God to tell them the glad tidings. Thus the apostle justifies himself in going to the Gentiles with the good news. Their own Scriptures prove the necessity of the very thing to which the Jew objected (1 Thessalonians 2:16). The Jews persistently opposed and persecuted Paul for preaching to the Gentiles, yet their great prophet, Isaiah, had said that the thing they condemned was beautiful. 'How beautiful are the feet of them that preach the gospel of peace'.

VERSE *16*

Alas! the Jew not only resisted the good news going to the Gentile, but they did not believe it themselves, as Isaiah says, 'Lord, who hath believed our report?' (Isaiah 53:1).

VERSE *17*

Thus the apostle concludes that the blessing comes by faith, and faith cometh by report and that report by the word of God. The word of God is the infallible authority for the report, and for believing the report. Hence, the great effort of Satan today to undermine the word of God, by calling in question its verbal inspiration.

VERSE 18

Moreover, the testimony of creation condemned the attitude of the Jew, their own Scriptures being a witness to the fact that, in creation, God is sending out a testimony to the ends of the habitable world (Psalm 19:4).

VERSE 19

Further, how can Israel plead that they did not know God had blessing for the Gentile, for Moses said, speaking of God's dealings with the nation, 'I will provoke you to jealousy by them that are no people, and by a foolish people will I anger you'. An implication that God would put Israel to shame by blessing the Gentile.

VERSE 20

Isaiah, too, is very plain for he says not only that the report must go out to the Gentile but that Jehovah would be found of the Gentiles who had not sought after Him, though Israel rejects the glad tidings in spite of God stretching out His hands to them in grace.

4. GRACE RESTORING ISRAEL ON THE FALL OF THE GENTILE

CHAPTER 11

The ninth chapter proves, not only that God's dealings in sovereign grace are perfectly consistent with the special promises to Israel, but, that the fulfilment of the promises is dependent upon grace.

The tenth chapter shows that Israel has, not only broken the law, but, rejected the gospel of God's grace, with the result that God turns to the Gentile and for the time being sets aside the nation of Israel that has stumbled and fallen.

The eleventh chapter shows that though Israel has stumbled and fallen, the nation is not cast away for ever. Moreover, it indicates that the Gentiles, towards whom God is acting in grace, will finally reject the grace of God, and that their fall from grace will become the occasion of Israel being restored to blessing.

THE ELECTION OF A REMNANT OF ISRAEL THE GREAT PROOF THAT THE NATION IS NOT CAST AWAY (11:1-6)

VERSE 1

The apostle has shown that the nation of Israel had, not only broken the law, but, according to prophecy, had rejected the glad tidings of grace and consequently, as a nation had fallen. The fall and scattering of the nation at once raises the question, 'Has God cast away His people?' The opening verses of this chapter set forth different reasons to show that this is far from the case.

First, the apostle himself was a proof that this failure of the nation does not necessarily involve that they are rejected forever. There can be no question that Paul by birth was an Israelite of the seed of Abraham, and that there had been no greater opponent of the gospel than himself, nevertheless he is chosen for blessing.

VERSES 2-4

Secondly, God will not cast away people whose evil was foreknown before He took them up.

Thirdly, the apostle shows that in the very darkest day of the nation's history God had reserved to Himself a remnant. In the days of Elijah, when the nation had rejected the message of God through the prophet, so low was the condition of the people that the prophet pleads with God against the nation. So thoroughly disheartened was Elijah, that he thought that he only was standing for God, and it seemed that he actually desired God to cut off the nation. He has to learn that however terrible their condition God had reserved to Himself seven thousand that had not bowed the knee to Baal.

VERSES 5-6

Fourthly, even as it was in the day of Elijah, so at the present time, when the nation as a whole is scattered because of their rejection of Christ, God still has 'a remnant according to the election of grace'. And if of grace, it is 'no more of works'. On the ground of works they had utterly broken down and had been rejected. On the ground of grace God has reserved a remnant in whom the nation will be restored.

WHILE A REMNANT FROM ISRAEL IS CHOSEN, THE NATION IS JUDICIALLY BLINDED (11:7-10)

VERSES 7-10

Rejecting Christ, and the grace of God proclaimed by the Holy Spirit through His servants, the nation falls into the spiritual blindness foretold by the prophet Isaiah. Wilfully rejecting Christ they can no longer see their need, or the grace of God that can meet that need.

So David foretells that their very privileges would become a snare to them. Boasting in their outward privileges they despise the grace of God. In result their eyes are darkened that they cannot see the goodness of God and their backs are bowed in bondage to their enemies.

THE FALL OF ISRAEL OPENS THE DOOR OF BLESSING TO THE GENTILES (11:11-15)

VERSES 11-15

If then Israel had rejected their Messiah and stumbled at the stumblingstone, was it simply that they should fall? Far be the thought, for God has purposes of blessing for the nation which will yet be carried out; in the meantime God uses their fall for the occasion of proclaiming salvation to the Gentiles. Moreover, if God proclaims salvation to the Gentiles, it is not only that the Gentiles may be blessed but, that through their blessing, Israel may be pro-voked to jealously and again turn to God.

Further, if the fall of Israel leads to the blessing of the Gentile world, how much more, when God restores Israel, will their fullness of blessing bring blessing to the wide world. If the casting away of the nation leads to the gospel of reconciliation going out to the world, then indeed, when they are received back into blessing as a nation, it will be life for the world. All the prophecies of millennial blessing for a world under the curse, await the restoration of Israel as the centre of blessing for the earth.

THE FAILURE OF THE GENTILES OPENS THE WAY FOR THE RESTORATION OF ISRAEL (11:16-29)

VERSES 16-19

The godly remnant of Israel at the present time is the first-fruit of the restored nation. If the firstfruit is holy, so will the lump be — the nation as a whole. If the root of the tree is holy, so are the branches. Israel is thus likened to an olive tree planted to produce fruit. Abraham was the root, the one to whom the promises of earthly blessing were made. The unbelieving Jews, while boasting in their con-nection with the tree of promise, were but dead branches, and, as such, were broken off.

But, as we have seen, the rejection of Israel becomes the occasion for bringing blessing to the Gentiles. The break-ing off of the natural branches becomes the occasion for grafting in branches from the wild olive, that they may partake of the earthly blessing connected with the root.

Nevertheless, let the Gentile beware of boasting against the Jew. The blessing which the Gentile comes into has its root in Abraham, the father of all that believe. The branches grafted into the tree cannot boast against the natural branches, because some were broken off.

VERSES 20-21

Let the Gentile then beware. It was because of *unbelief* that Israel was cut off, and it is only through *faith* in God that the Gentiles come into blessing. Faith makes everything of God, let the Gentiles beware of the highmindedness that makes something of self lest they, too, fall into unbelief. If God spared not the natural branches because of their unbelief we may be sure He will not spare the Gentiles if they fall into unbelief.

VERSES 22-25

Thus, in God's dealings with Israel and the Gentiles, we see the goodness and the severity of God. God has acted in severity towards unbelieving Israel, and in goodness toward the Gentile. But His 'goodness' will cease towards the Gentiles if they fall into unbelief; and God's severity can cease toward Israel if they repent of their unbelief. In this case the fall of the Gentiles will become the occasion for the restoration of Israel. If wild olive branches can be grafted into the olive tree so can the natural branches. This indeed is what will happen, for the blindness that has come upon Israel is only blindness in part. The nation is not blinded nevermore to see, nor fallen never to be restored, nor cast off never to be received. The time of their casting off will end when the fullness of the Gentiles has been brought into blessing.

VERSES 26-27

Thus the time is coming when Israel, as a whole, will be saved from their enemies. The time of their deliverance awaits the coming of Christ out of Zion as the Deliverer.

Then the nation will turn from their iniquities and God will take away their sins.

Verses 28-29

As concerning the gospel, they are at this moment enemies, that the Gentiles may be blessed. But, however much they have failed they are still the elect nation, beloved for the father's sake to whom the promises were made: and the gifts and calling of God are without repentance.

The failure of Jew and Gentile shuts up all the world to the mercy of God (11:30-32)

The way of God in bestowing His gifts and accomplishing His call, is to take occasion by man's unbelief to show forth His mercy. He concludes all in unbelief that He may have mercy upon all. Thus the great truth is established that we owe all blessing to the sovereign grace of God.

The doxology that celebrates the resources and wisdom of God (11:33-36)

If the sovereign purposes of God in blessing, are worked out, not only in spite of man's failure, but through the very failure of man, we can only say, 'O the depth of riches both of the wisdom and knowledge of God'. Both the judgements of God in regard to the failure of man, and the ways of God in carrying out His purposes for the blessing of men, make manifest that there are depth of riches in His wisdom and knowledge that are unsearchable, and therefore past finding out by man. If they are to be known in any measure it can only be by revelation, and in the practical carrying out of His judgements and ways with men.

All God's wisdom and knowledge has its source in Himself. No-one has been His counsellor. All blessing for the universe has its source in God — it is 'of Him'; it is all brought to pass 'through Him', and will all return 'to Him' for His glory. Therefore the apostle concludes 'to whom be glory for ever'.

To understand the teaching of this chapter it is important to see that the church is not the subject. The chapter is occupied with God's way with Israel and the Gentiles. The church is composed of believers taken out from Israel and the Gentiles, and therefore has nothing to do with Jew or Gentile as such. The blessings of the church are heavenly: the blessings of Israel and the nations are earthly.

Difficulties arise if we do not see that, quite apart from the calling out of the church, God has His ways with Israel and the Gentiles, and that, in the government of God, we are living in the times of the Gentiles, that is the period during which Israel is set aside as a nation and the government of the world has been given to the Gentiles. In this government the Gentiles have broken down and used the power that God has committed to them without reference to God. Today we see the nations fast throwing off all fear of God, with the result that they in turn will be set aside, and Israel be restored to her place of pre-eminence in the government of the world.

DIVISION 4

PRACTICAL EXHORTATIONS

Chapters 12 – 15:13

1. INTRODUCTORY

Having, in the first part of the epistle, very fully presented the truths that establish the believer in right relations with God, the apostle, in this fresh division, sets before us the conduct that is suited to these relationships. It is evident that doctrine must precede practice. In other words, the truth of the relationship must be known, before we can act in a way suited to the relationship.

Chapter eleven closes with a burst of praise for the sovereign mercy of God that acts in grace towards all — Jew and Gentile alike. The practical exhortations that follow are addressed to those who have been blessed by this sovereign grace. We are not exhorted to a right course of conduct in order to obtain the blessing, but because we are blessed. We exhort our children to obedience, and the conduct that becomes children, not to make them children, but because they are children.

It will be noticed that these practical exhortations fall into three distinct classes.

First, in chapter twelve, the exhortations present the conduct consistent with the truth that believers form one body in Christ.

Secondly, in chapter thirteen, the exhortations set forth the conduct proper to the believers in connection with the kingdom of man through which they are passing.

Thirdly, in chapters fourteen to fifteen verse 13 the conduct suited to believers as belonging to the kingdom of God.

2. CONDUCT IN RELATION TO ONE ANOTHER IN THE CHRISTIAN CIRCLE

CHAPTER 12

The exhortations as to our practical conduct, of necessity commence with the inner circle — the Christian circle. If our manner of life is not right in this circle, we shall not understand the conduct suited to the Christian as he comes into touch with the world he is passing through.

In verses 1-5 we are exhorted as to the practice consistent with our relationships to God and to one another. Then, in verses 6-8, there is brought before us different forms of service, and from verse 9 to the end of the chapter, the moral characteristics that should mark those who serve the Lord.

OUR RELATIONS TO GOD AND TO ONE ANOTHER (12:1-5)
VERSE 1

The apostle appeals to believers on the ground of the mercies of God by which they have been so richly blessed — the mercies that have been unfolded to us in the first eleven chapters. Seeing that we have been so richly blessed it becomes us to present our bodies a living sacrifice, holy, acceptable unto God. This is our only intelligent service. In pressing the deep need of governing our spirits, and having our affections held in check, we may be in danger of thinking this is all, and that we can be careless as to the way we use our bodies. Here, then, it is our bodies that are to be yielded to God. Our feet to walk in the path of obedience, our hands employed in His service, our tongues to speak as a witness for God. This will involve sacrifice, for the natural inclination is to use the body to carry out the will of the flesh. To restrain the flesh involves the sacrifice of much that nature desires. The body presented to God is not only a sacrifice, but it is a *living* sacrifice. We may present our money, and our goods, but such gifts, however right in their place, are not 'living'. With such gifts there may be, at the same time, much self-indulgence of the body. Moreover it is to be presented as a 'holy' sacrifice. For God's service there is required not only a living body, but a 'holy' body. Only as the body is held in holiness will the sacrifice be acceptable.

VERSE 2

Having presented the body to God we are warned against the ever present danger of the world. The world is at enmity with God and lieth in the wicked one. We are to beware of adopting its godless ways and speech. But, further, we are to be transformed.

We are not only to beware of being formed like it, but we are to be altogether different from it. This transformation can only be by the renewing of the mind. It is not a mere outward transformation by the adoption of some peculiar religious dress, such as that of a monk or nun, which, however plain, only calls attention to self. The difference between the world and the believer is to be displayed, not simply in dress, but in manner and speech and spirit, as the result of having a different *mind*. The outward change is the result of an inward change of thought. We may raise endless questions as to what is right in dress and manner of life, but the inward change — the renewing of the mind — would settle a thousand questions as to what is the good and acceptable and perfect will of God.

VERSE 3

We are next exhorted to have right and sober thoughts as to ourselves. We are warned against thinking of ourselves more highly than we ought to think. The apostle, in another epistle, speaks of those who are 'vainly puffed up', indicating that behind high thoughts of self there lurks the vanity of the flesh (Colossians 2:18). The Corinthian saints were evidently thinking too highly of themselves. They were 'puffed up for one against another' (1 Corinthians 4:6). The vanity that makes us think highly of ourselves will lead us to disparage others in the effort to exalt ourselves.

We are to think soberly, recognising our limitations, and that God only gives the measure of faith needed to perform the service to which we are called. If we attempt to do another's work we shall soon find that we have neither the needed grace nor faith.

VERSES 4-5

To act rightly we must understand our relation to one another. For this reason the apostle touches upon the truth of the church comprised of many members but forming one body. Being formed into one body we are members one of another, and cannot rightly act independently of one another. All true service and conduct, of which the apostle is about to speak, flows not from our being members of a meeting, or from being members of some religious society, of which Scripture knows nothing, but from the fact that we are members one of another as forming one body in Christ. To carry out the service of the Lord we have not to band ourselves together into a society under some human head, but to recognise that we have already been formed into one body of which Christ is the Head.

To sum up the exhortations of the opening verses: we are first exhorted to hold the body for God; secondly, to refuse the world; thirdly, to have sober thoughts of ourselves; and finally to have a right appreciation of our relations to one another.

DIFFERENT FORMS OF SERVICE (12:6-8)

It is plain that the exhortations of verses 1-5, present the necessary preparation for the different forms of service of which the apostle proceeds to speak. Seven characters of service are brought before us. They are called gifts, though clearly they include not only the public gifts for the church, but also the more private forms of service. Whatever the service, it can only be rightly exercised according to the grace given. It follows that in the exercise of the gift we are dependent upon the Giver.

1   **Prophecy** : We know from 1 Corinthians 14:1-3 that of all spiritual gifts prophesying is the one most to be desired, and further, that this gift implies 'edification and exhortation and comfort'. Here we are reminded that the gift is to be used in faith. We are to beware of taking any credit to ourselves, as if the mere exercise of the gift could effect any good in the hearer. It is to be exercised in the faith that counts upon God to apply the word.

2   **Ministry** : The word implies the service of love to the saints which may take many forms other than public speaking. But, whatever the service, let the servant see that he occupies himself with it, and not

attempt that to which he is not called, and for which he has no divinely given fitness.

3 **Teaching** : Teaching would seem to have more in view the orderly exposition of Scripture and its doctrines.

4 **Exhortation** : Exhortation would appear to be the pressing home of some great truth in a practical way. Again, those who have these gifts are to give themselves to them, and not attempt a form of service for which they have no gift.

5 **Giving** : The one who is in a position to serve by giving, whatever form the gift may take, is to be careful to give without ostentation or parade.

6 **Leading** : It is not a little striking that leading is placed among the services that have been given to the saints. The leader is not necessarily gifted to teach or preach, nor, on the other hand, is the teacher and preacher necessarily a leader. The leader is one who, by his wisdom and experience, is fitted to guide the people of God. He is to exercise his gift with the diligence that uses thought and care in his guidance.

7 **Showing mercy** : This is the happy service that expresses itself in acts of kindness and consideration for those in special need. It is not to be exercised grudgingly, but with the cheerfulness that can only come from the unselfish love that finds its pleasure in serving others.

THE MORAL CHARACTERISTICS THAT SHOULD MARK BELIEVERS (12:9-21)

Having set before us some of the many forms of service we may be privileged to exercise by divinely given grace, we

THE EPISTLE TO THE ROMANS

are now exhorted as to the conduct and spirit, which should mark the Lord's people and without which every form of service will be marred.

VERSE 9

The first three exhortations plainly have reference to ourselves personally. We are each to see that our love is unfeigned, that we treat evil with abhorrence, and that we are devoted to that which is good. Alas! It is easy to feign love, while professing to act in love. Joab can kiss the man he is about to murder, and Judas can kiss His Master in order to betray Him. The flesh can act like Israel of old, of whom it is written, 'with their mouth they show much love, but their heart goeth after their covetousness' (Ezekiel 33:31). Unfeigned love, is an unselfish love that thinks of the good of others.

Love and abhorrence of evil will ever be found together. Says the Psalmist, 'Ye that love the LORD, hate evil' (Psalm 97:10). A false charity may ignore evil under the plea of love, and even treat evil doctrine as to the Lord of little account. Unfeigned love will lead us to abhor evil without ignoring the good. In our abhorrence of evil we may overlook much good; or, in seeking to cleave to the good we may compromise with evil.

VERSE 10

The next two exhortations concern our relations with one another. We are to be 'kindly affectioned one to another with brotherly love; in honour preferring one another'. Our affection to one another should flow from our relationship as 'brethren', and not simply because of some quality which may be attractive or advantageous to us; brotherly love would make us ready to let others have honour rather than grasping it for ourselves.

Verse 11

Three exhortations follow that more directly have the Lord in view. In our service to the Lord we are to be diligent with a holy zeal that resists slothfulness. Zeal, however, may degenerate into mere outward activity, so we are exhorted to fervency of spirit that has the Lord before us as the motive of the service.

Verse 12

The following three exhortations refer to the trials by the way. The hope of the coming glory will sustain us in trial and enable us to be patient under the trial; while in prayer, that casts all upon the Lord, we shall find support in the trial.

Verse 13

Then we have two exhortations as to the needs of the Lord's people. We are exhorted to meet the 'necessities' of the poor, and to be ready to show hospitality.

Verse 14

In reference to persecution that we may meet, Christianity would teach us to bless, where nature would retaliate by rendering evil for evil.

Verse 15

In connection with the changing circumstances of life we should be ready to rejoice with those who rightly rejoice, and weep with those in sorrow.

Verse 16

As to social questions we are to beware of letting the spirit of the world into the Christian circle, that would esteem people according to their birth, wealth, or social position. We are to have the same respect for the poor brother as for the rich, and to refuse the natural vanity of the flesh that thinks much of 'high things'. It is our privilege and honour, as Christians, to be found 'going along with the lowly' (N.Tr.). Nor is it enough to associate with the lowly; we need to have the lowly mind. Therefore, the apostle adds, 'Be not wise in your own eyes' (N.Tr.).

VERSES *17-18*

As regards our relations with men of the world, and in connection with our earthly calling, we are to beware of bringing reproach upon our profession by recompensing evil for evil. We are to exercise the needed forethought to provide for our necessities in a way that is honest in the sight of all men. As far as it depends upon us we are to live at peace with all.

VERSES *19-21*

Finally we are exhorted as to showing a right Christian spirit in connection with wrongs that we may have to meet. In a world like this we may have to suffer wrong, face insults and opposition, and that even from professing Christians; but come from what quarter it may, we are not to attempt to avenge ourselves, but quietly give way to wrath. Naturally we should seek to revenge a wrong, but this the Lord does not entrust to us. Vengeance, He keeps in His own hands, for He has said, 'Vengeance *is mine*: I will repay saith the Lord' (Psalm 94:1). Our part is, under all circumstances, to maintain the Christian spirit and seek to win our enemies by showing kindness to those who have acted wrongly toward us. Thus acting we shall not be overcome of evil, but overcome evil with good.

3.　CONDUCT IN CONNECTION WITH THE WORLD

CHAPTER 13

The exhortations in chapter 12 have in view the conduct that is becoming to believers in connection with the Christian circle. The exhortations of chapter 13 instruct us as to the right attitude, and conduct, of Christians towards the world they are passing through.

First, we are instructed as to our attitude towards those set in authority in the world (verses 1-7).

Secondly, there is set before us the spirit in which we should act toward all men (verses 8-10).

Thirdly, the apostle presents the practical walk that becomes the children of light in the midst of a world of darkness (verses 11-14).

THE CHRISTIAN'S ATTITUDE TOWARDS THOSE SET IN AUTHORITY (13:1-7)

VERSE 1

Already we have been told not to be conformed to the world, marked as it is by lust and pride, but, by the renewing of the mind, to exhibit a character that is in entire contrast to the man of the world. Nevertheless, the

Christian is to recognise that government has been established in the world, and that the authority to govern is
from God. This government was instituted after the flood,
when Noah was definitely told that 'Whoso sheddeth
man's blood by man shall his blood be shed' (Genesis 9:6).

It is important to see the bearing of this Scripture. It definitely asserts that the *authority to govern* has been given
by God. It does not say that the particular individuals
who exercise the authority are of God, or that the way
they may use their authority is of God. Those who exercise authority may be, and often are, thoroughly wicked
men, who may abuse the power for their own ends. The
fact however remains, that the authority they wield has
been instituted of God.

Recognising that authority to govern is an ordinance of
God, the only right course for the believer is to submit to
those in authority.

As strangers and pilgrims, believers are only passing
through the world, and as such it would be wholly incon-
sistent for them to meddle with its government. They are
called out of the world; they are not called to put right a
world that has cast out Christ. It is no part of their business to oppose the government that exists, nor to take part
in electing what they might rightly judge to be a better
form of government. Their one business is to be subject.

VERSE 2

To oppose any particular ruler is to oppose the authority
established by God. To resist what is of God is to bring
oneself under condemnation.

VERSES 3-4

God has given men authority in order to restrain evil and
protect good. It follows that those in authority are not a

terror to good works but to evil. Would we then walk without fear of authority, let us refrain from evil. Whether he is aware of it or not, the one in authority is a minister of God to exercise judgement upon the evil doer; and, in spite of the fact that men often pervert government to their own ends, it will be found in the main, that in the mercy of God the very worst governments seek to restrain evil.

Verse 5

Knowing then God's mind for the Christian in relation to the world, we must needs be subject, not only to escape punishment for doing wrong, but also to maintain a good conscience toward God. Obeying God's word, and walking in subjection, we shall find that the one in authority is God's minister to the Christian for good, and the minister of God to revenge and deal with evil.

Verses 6-7

Those in authority being God's officers to exercise government we are to pay tribute when tribute is due, and custom to whom custom is due, and yield fear and honour to whom due. It is not for the believer to raise questions as to how the tribute is spent. The use of the tribute and custom is no part of our responsibility. Other Scripture will show that if the government requires the believer to act in plain conflict with the word of God, he is to obey God rather than men, but even so it will be in suffering rather than resisting.

THE BELIEVER'S CONDUCT IN RELATION TO ALL MEN (13:8-10)

Verses 8-10

In these verses we are exhorted as to the right conduct of the believer towards all men, whether believers or unbelievers. Being our conduct towards all, the law is brought in, rather than the higher standard of Christianity. We are to owe no man anything except to love. In showing love we shall fulfil the law, for the whole law is comprehended in this saying, 'Thou shalt love thy neighbour as thyself'. Love worketh no evil. Love will not kill, nor steal, nor bear false witness. It is true that apart altogether from love, a man refrains from killing or stealing for fear of consequences, and yet easily slips into bearing false witness. Only love will refrain from bearing false witness against our brother. Apart from love we may rake up something against a brother that we know has been judged and owned and done with, and thus, by an idle word, destroy his reputation. In the Christian circle everyone's reputation should be safe from slander. 'Love worketh no ill to his neighbour', but malice does, and giving way to malice we fall beneath the law, not to speak of the higher claims of Christianity.

THE WALK THAT BECOMES THE CHILDREN OF LIGHT IN A WORLD OF DARKNESS (13:11-14)
VERSE 11

Believers are to recognise and submit to authority knowing that the authorities 'that exist are set up by God' (verse 1, N.Tr.) We are also to walk righteously toward all men (verses 8-10). Nevertheless, we are to remember that the world is in darkness or ignorance of God, and that as believers we have been brought into the light of the knowledge of God and are to walk according to the light.

The apostle appeals to believers as 'knowing the time'. The world may be full of misgivings, their hearts failing them through fear and for looking after those things which are coming on the earth; but this only proves that the world does not know the time. We know that all the confusion and unrest in the world only tells us that the day of glory is not far off. We are called to glory. 'We rejoice in hope of the glory of God'. 'We are saved by hope'. (Romans 8:30; 5:2; 8:24). And we know that the full salvation for which we wait is nearer than when we believed. Knowing the time — that the dawn is breaking — it is high time to awaken from sleep.

VERSES 12-14

'The night is far spent the day is at hand'. When Christ was present in the world He could say, 'As long as I am in the world, I am the light of the world' (John 9:5). In those wonderful days, He proved that He alone could dispel the darkness by declaring the love of the Father. He proved too, that He had the power and the grace to remove all the evil that the darkness had brought in. He relieved man of every pressure, met every need, and delivered from the power of the Prince of darkness. Hunger and want, pain and sickness, sorrow and death, all fled in His presence. Alas! Men loved darkness rather than light. They loved the sins which, in the presence of the light, troubled their consciences. Being unable to pursue their sins and gratify their lusts in the presence of the light, they put out the light of the world. Christ is gone, and His absence leaves the world in darkness. As they could not put up with the light of His presence, they have to put up with the wars, the want, the sorrow and the distress which results from sin, during the night of His absence.

But the day is at hand — the day when He will return in glory to reign over the earth; when all evil will be put under His feet and Satan's power subdued. In that day, 'The ransomed of the Lord shall return, and come to Zion with songs and everlasting joy upon their heads: they shall obtain joy and gladness, and sorrow and sighing shall flee away' (Isaiah 35:10).

In view of this day — this glorious day — the apostle presses upon us four exhortations:–

First, 'let us therefore cast off the works of darkness'. All the works that characterise men walking in ignorance of God are to be cast aside. In another epistle the apostle describes those living in darkness as 'serving divers lusts and pleasures, living in malice and envy, hateful, and hating one another' (Titus 3:3).

Secondly, the apostle says, 'let us put on the armour of light'. All that marks the coming day — the day when Christ reigns — the submission and obedience to the Lord (verses 1-7), the righteousness that owes no man anything (verse 8), the love that worketh no evil to his neighbour (verse 10), are to be put on by the believer as protective armour against the darkness.

Thirdly, the apostle says, 'As in the day, let us walk becomingly' (N.Tr.). In spirit in the day we are yet, as to fact, in the night. The world in darkness may give itself up to 'rioting and drunkenness', 'chambering and wantonness', 'strife and envying'; but the Christian is to have no part in such things. This should call for the deepest exercise, for we may indeed keep clear of the grosser evils of darkness — its drunkenness and lasciviousness and yet fall into strife and envying. Have we not too often allowed ourselves to be drawn into strife, and given way to envying? Does not the apostle James warn us that 'bitter envying and strife' in our hearts is the root cause of every scene of disorder and strife in the people of God. 'For' he says, 'where envying and strife is, there is confusion and every evil work' (James 3:14-16).

Fourthly, we are exhorted to 'put on the Lord Jesus Christ' and 'not take forethought for the flesh to fulfil its lusts'. Not only are we to have done with the things of darkness, but to put on the character of Christ, and thus be invested with the beauty of the One Who is coming to reign. It is to become evident that we walk in subjection to the Lord, and are marked by the graces of Jesus Christ. Thus we shall become a witness during the night of His absence to the One who will usher in the day. Instead of taking thought of the flesh, and how to gratify its lusts, we are to take thought of Jesus, and seek to shine in His beauty.

> *Lord Jesus! Thy glory and beauty*
> *Have drawn our hearts captive up there;*
> *Then here let the garments that suit Thee*
> *Be only the garments we wear.*

4.　CONDUCT IN RELATION TO THE LORD'S KINGDOM

CHAPTERS 14 - 15:13

We have seen that in chapter 12 the exhortations to believers are mainly in view of their relationships to one another as members of the one body. In chapter 13 the exhortations have in view our conduct in relation to the world we are passing through. In chapter fourteen to fifteen verse 13 the exhortations are in connection with the Lord, and relate to our conduct as subjects in His kingdom.

This section of the epistle commences with speaking of the spirit in which we should receive one another, and ends with exhortations that, if carried out would bind us together in joy and peace. The apostle is not speaking of assembly reception, but of receiving one another — one individual receiving another individual in ordinary Christian intercourse. It is important to see the true bearing of this passage, as it has been so often misused to support the false ideas that, because a person is a Christian, and in that sense has been received of God, we are bound to receive such into assembly fellowship apart from their associations and spiritual condition.

172

In our intercourse with one another, we are to remember that we are subjects in the kingdom of God (14:17) and that each one is responsible to the Lord who rules over His kingdom. In this kingdom, some may be weak in the faith and some strong (14:1; 15:1); but whether 'weak' or 'strong', both are responsible to the Lord. Therefore, in matters in which no moral question is concerned, or in which there is no direct disobedience to the word of God, each must be left free to act before the Lord without interference from one another.

The apostle refers to two matters of this character — the question of eating, or refraining from eating, meats; and the question of observance, or non-observance, of certain days. Such questions very naturally had a prominent place in the apostle's day when so many of the converts were from amongst the Jews, who would find it difficult to rid their minds of the prejudices formed by their ancient religion in which so much was made of meats and the observance of days. The Gentile believers would more readily leave such things behind, seeing that the idolatrous systems that they had been connected with were wholly false.

But such questions were not to interfere with Christian intercourse, but rather call forth Christian forbearance.

The weak are not those who are tampering with evil, or walking in disobedience to the word, but rather those who were not in the full liberty of Christianity — those who may be very legal as to minor matters, and thus not only have a tender conscience, but even a morbid conscience.

CHAPTER 14 VERSES 1-2

The weak in the faith then are not to be shunned; they are to be received. Nevertheless the reception of such is not to be used for the determining of mere questions. The one received must not think that his reception involves the reception of his particular views as to meats or days. Furthermore, those who receive are not to take occasion by receiving one with a conscience as to these things, to interfere with his conscientious convictions before the Lord. One believeth that he may eat all things; another, that the apostle describes as weak, believes that it is right to eat herbs only.

VERSES 3-4

The apostle instructs us that, in such matters there is to be mutual forbearance. For this he gives three reasons. First, God has received both the weak and the strong. His reception of us did not depend upon our eating or not eating certain meats. Secondly, in such matters to our own Master we stand or fall and we are not to judge another man's service. Thirdly, the Lord is able to sustain us and make us to stand even if in such matters we are weak in the faith.

VERSES 5-8

The apostle includes also the question of regarding or not regarding special days. His argument supposes that whatever view is taken, whether of days or meats, each one is acting as before the Lord. None of us live to ourselves but to the Lord. It is well to see that the apostle is not speaking of the Lord's day. The observance of the first day of the week as the Lord's day has the sanction of Scripture and is not left as an open matter (See John 20:19; Acts 20:7; 1 Corinthians 16:2; Revelation 1:10).

VERSES 9-12

Christ has established His claim over us by dying and rising again that as the living Lord He might rule over both dead and living. The Lord is the Judge and it is before His judgement seat we shall all stand. Each one is responsible to give an account of himself to God.

Thus in the first twelve verses we are warned against slighting one another's conscience before the Lord, ignoring the Lord's rights over each one or interfering with our individual responsibilities to the Lord.

VERSES 13-18

Hitherto the apostle has shown us that plain duty would preserve us from interfering with one another in the matter of meats and days. Now he shows there is another motive that would keep us from judging one another in such matters; we are to walk *according to love* (verse 15). Moved by considerations of love for our brother, we should be careful not to put any stumbling block in his way.

Paul was fully persuaded that no meat in itself was unclean, but if to eat meat would give a brother a bad conscience, it would become an occasion of defilement to him. We are to be careful then not to use our liberty in the endeavour to persuade a brother to do something about which he has a conscience. We are persuading him to act beyond his faith and as far as the bearing of our act goes we are leading him to violate his conscience and thus drive him from Christ.

Thus the liberty of Christianity which we may rightly enjoy, may become an occasion for stumbling others and thus be evil spoken of.

The kingdom of God is not characterised by meats and drinks, but by righteousness, peace and joy in the Holy Spirit. These are moral characteristics of the kingdom to be enjoyed now by the believer in the power of the Spirit. They will be universally enjoyed when the kingdom is set up in power. These are the qualities to be pursued by both 'weak' and 'strong'. These things are acceptable to God and approved by men. The effort to impose my liberty on another, if it offends his weak conscience, is condemned by God and man.

VERSES 19-23

The apostle has exhorted us to walk according to love and not to stumble our brother. Now he exhorts us to follow peace and things wherewith we may edify one another. To seek to persuade a weak brother to do that which may give him a bad conscience is, in its tendency, to destroy the work of God in his soul and become an occasion of stumbling to him. It is better not to eat flesh and drink wine, if by so doing we offend and damage our brother.

Have we faith to do certain things, let us have it before God. To be strong in faith is right, but we are not to attempt to lead another to do something about which he is doubtful. It may lead him into a path which is not of faith; and whatsoever cannot be done in faith is sin.

CHAPTER 15 VERSES 1-2

The first thirteen verses of chapter fifteen conclude the subject of chapter fourteen — the conduct suited to believers as being in the kingdom of God. It will be noticed that the four leading exhortations of this portion are introduced with the word 'Let'. First the apostle says, *'Let* not him that eateth despise him that eateth not' (14:3) and we are thus exhorted to *mutual forbearance* in matters where no association with evil, or disobedience to the word, is involved. The second great exhortation is introduced with the words *'Let* us not therefore judge one another any more' (14:13) and he presses us to walk charitably, or as it should be translated, *'according to love'*. Thirdly he says, 'Let us therefore follow after the things which make for *peace*' (14:19). Finally, in the second verse of chapter fifteen the apostle says, 'Let every one of us *please his neighbour for his good* to edification'.

Thus as subjects in the kingdom of God, we are to be marked by mutual forbearance, love, peace and the unselfishness that loses sight of self in order to please others for their good.

VERSES 3-7

For our encouragement, the apostle brings Christ before us as the perfect example of One who pleased not Himself. This indeed was so different to the way of the world that it brought Him into reproach.

Further, we have not only the example of Christ but the encouragement of Scripture. For whatsoever things were written aforetime were written for our learning that we through patience and comfort might have hope.

Moreover we have not only the comfort of Scripture, but we have the support of God Himself, the God of endurance and encouragement to sustain us in a way that is suited to the kingdom.

All these exhortations have in view the great end, that we should 'be like minded one toward another according to Christ', in order that we may 'with one mind and one mouth glorify God, even the Father of our Lord Jesus Christ'. The apostle clearly shows that in order to glorify God with one mind it is absolutely essential that we should be 'like minded one toward another'. We see these two things marking the saints in Pentecostal days. We read that 'they lifted up their voices with one accord to God'. Then we are told that these believers, who could glorify God with 'one mind', were 'of one heart and of one soul'. They were one-minded toward God because they were likeminded one toward another (Acts 4:24, 32). Alas! The unity of those early days has passed away. We live in a day of ruin when the utmost confusion prevails in Christendom. Even amongst those who have sought to walk in obedience to the word of God for a day of ruin, we see how constantly the devil has succeeded in bringing in what the apostle James speaks of as 'Envying and strife', leading to 'confusion and every evil work'. If, however, we cannot gather all the saints together, is it not possible for a few to be found 'likeminded one toward another' and thus glorifying God with one mind. These Scriptures show how this is still possible.

Let us notice that when the apostle speaks of being 'likeminded one toward another', he immediately adds the words 'according to Christ Jesus'. It is possible to be likeminded according to nature, or the flesh and entirely miss the mind of Christ. To be likeminded according to Christ, we must be marked by the characteristics that the apostle has been bringing before us, the mutual forbearance, love, peace and unselfishness that forgets self in seeking to please others for their good. Then indeed we shall 'with one mind and one mouth glorify God, even the Father of our Lord Jesus Christ'. How different our lives would be, and what wonderful times of worship we should have, when come together to remember the Lord, if by grace we were all 'likeminded one toward another'.

VERSE 8

The apostle concludes these practical exhortations by referring to the ministry of Christ which has in view the purpose of God to bind together Jew and Gentile through Christ, that they with one mind may glorify God. The assembly at Rome was probably a mixed company of Jewish and Gentile believers and the danger was that each might bring national prejudices into the assembly and thus disturb the harmony of the whole.

The practical bearing of chapters fourteen to fifteen verse 13 is to show that believers can only walk together as each one is subject to the Lord. There were matters of conscience as to meats and drinks and days and we are not to override conscience. Mere reasoning and persuasion will not solve these questions nor enable those to walk together who differ as to these things. It is only as each one is individually near the Lord, and keeps near the Lord, that we shall be able to walk in peace with one another. How easily can any one of us, if out of touch with the Lord, break up the harmony of an assembly.

Now the great object of the ministry of the Lord is to bind together Jew and Gentile, who naturally are entirely antagonistic in the worship and praise of God. This we know will be accomplished in the millennial day. In the meantime believers from amongst Jews and Gentiles are brought together in one body on heavenly ground, where all national distinctions disappear. It is obvious we shall find nothing in the Old Testament as to the church; nevertheless there are many glorious prophecies that foretell the day when Jews and Gentiles will be bound together in the recognition and praise of God.

In order to show that one great end of the ministry of the Lord is to confirm the promises of worldwide blessing made to the fathers, the apostle quotes from the Psalms, the law and the prophets.

VERSE 9

The first quotation is from Psalm 18:49. The promise had been made to Abraham that 'in thee shall all families of the earth be blessed'. In order to confirm this and similar promises to the fathers, the Lord shows mercy and bears witness to God among the Gentiles.

Verse 10

The second quotation is from the law — Deuteronomy 32:43 — and tells us that not only the Gentiles will sing unto God but that they will do so 'with His people' — Israel.

Verse 11

The third quotation, from Psalm 117:1, is an appeal to Jew and Gentile to join together in the praise of the Lord.

Verse 12

The last quotation from the prophets — Isaiah 11:10 — proves that Christ Himself is the bond that will unite Jew and Gentile together. He arises amongst the Jews — the root of Jesse — to reign over the Gentiles and 'in Him shall the nations hope' (N.Tr.).

Verse 13

On the ground of this mercy and grace that flows out to the Gentiles and will yet bring Jew and Gentile together in the coming kingdom, the apostle commends believers to the God of hope that they might be filled with joy and peace in believing and abound in hope through the power of the Holy Spirit who is the Earnest of the coming glory.

With the prospect of the coming glory before us we should be lifted above all questions of meats and drinks and observance of days and in the joy of the prospect of the coming glory we should enjoy peace amongst ourselves.

PERSONAL APPEALS AND SALUTATIONS

Chapter 15:14 – 16:27

In this final division of the epistle the apostle makes a personal appeal to the saints at Rome in which he refers to the special ministry committed to him in order to explain why he ventures to write to those whom he had never seen. Then having desired their prayers, he closes with salutations.

THE MINISTRY OF THE APOSTLE IN SPIRITUAL THINGS (15:14-24)

VERSE 14

He introduces the subject of his ministry with that Christian love and lowliness that delights to recognise goodness and knowledge in others. If then he had exhorted and admonished them in his epistle, it was not to imply that they were unable to admonish one another.

VERSES 15-16

He had written rather as putting them in mind of truths with which they were acquainted. Ministry then is not only to enlighten us as to truth but is also largely concerned with pressing home upon our souls and applying to our particular circumstances, the truths that we have already received.

THE EPISTLE TO THE ROMANS

Moreover in writing to Gentile believers the apostle was carrying out the special grace given to him in order that as the servant of Jesus Christ he should minister the gospel to the Gentiles. The end of such ministry being that the Gentiles who believed, being set apart from the world by the Holy Spirit, might be an acceptable sacrifice unto God.

Verse 17

Wherever this blessed result was brought about by the apostle he had whereof he could glory in Jesus Christ. But this glorying was in things pertaining to God; not in things that were gain to him in the flesh.

Verses 18-21

Having spoken of the special grace given to him, and the object of this grace, the apostle with becoming modesty, refers briefly to the way in which he had sought to carry out this ministry. Christ had other servants who had been used by the Lord for the blessing of souls, but the apostle would not judge of their work. He refers only to what Christ had wrought by himself, his preaching being accompanied with mighty signs and wonders in the power of the Holy Spirit. The apostle had sought to avoid places where Christ was already named, lest he should build upon another man's foundation. His aim was to preach to those who had not heard according to the word in Isaiah 52:15: 'To whom he was not spoken of, they shall see: and they that have not heard shall understand'.

Verses 22-24

This gospel work had hindered Paul from coming to Rome but now having finished his work in the district from Jerusalem to Illyracum, and having a great desire to see the saints in Rome, he purposed to come to them on his way to Spain.

THE MINISTRY OF THE APOSTLE IN TEMPORAL THINGS (15:25-27)

In the meantime he had another form of ministry to fulfil. There were saints at Jerusalem in poverty and it had pleased the brethren in Macedonia and Achaia to make a certain contribution for them and Paul was anxious to take this contribution to Jerusalem. The saints of Macedonia while willingly contributing to the need of their brethren in Jerusalem, were nonetheless debtors to them, seeing they had received spiritual blessing from the Jerusalem saints. This service being completed Paul purposed to visit the saints at Rome.

THE APOSTLE'S DESIRE FOR THE PRAYERS OF THE SAINTS (15:30-33)

When the apostle came to Rome he was confident that it would be in the fullness of Christ. For this very reason he desired the prayers of these saints and not only as individuals but that they would 'strive together' in prayer. The apostle seems to feel that in going to Jerusalem he would encounter the hostility of the Jews that were unbelieving. Moreover, apparently he thought it possible that the believing Jews with their strong prejudices, might refuse the help sent from Gentile believers. He desires therefore that his service in this respect might be acceptable.

Finally, he desires that by the will of God he might come to them with joy, and that his coming might be for mutual refreshment. In the meantime he commends them to God. Already he had committed them to the God of endurance and encouragement (verse 5); then to the God of hope (verse 13); now he prays that the God of peace might be with them all.

COMMENDATIONS AND SALUTATIONS (CHAPTER 16)

Though the apostle had never visited the saints at Rome, many individuals were known to him and he delights to remember them. Love shines in all these salutations though it is a discriminating love. Though so highly gifted as an apostle, in the largeness of his heart he delights to recognise others in the service of the Lord. With the apostle there was no unworthy pettiness that in a spirit of jealousy, seeks to exalt self by belittling others. Nor does he think so highly of himself as to treat any kindness as simply his due. On the contrary, he recalls with gratitude every little bit of service to himself (verses 2-4).

VERSES 1-2

He first commends Phebe, who he describes not simply as a sister, but as 'our sister'. She had served the assembly at Cenchrea, been a succourer of many and the apostle adds, 'of myself also'. They are desired to receive her and assist her, especially remembering that she had assisted others. In all this they were to act in the Name of the Lord as becomes saints.

VERSES 3-5

Greetings were sent to Priscilla and her husband Aquila. They were by trade tentmakers, even as the apostle and may have helped Paul in his trade (Acts 18:3): but here he dwells upon the fact that they had been his helpers in Christ Jesus. Moreover they had risked their own necks to save his life and for this he not only himself gives them thanks, but also all the assemblies of the Gentiles. There evidently was an assembly meeting in their house to whom he sends greetings.

Paul describes Epænetus as his well-beloved, and we see in this case as in many others, that the apostle does not wait until a brother has fallen asleep to express his affection for him. If he loves a brother, he tells him so.

If you have a friend worth loving,
Love him. Yes, and let him know
That you love him, e'er life's evening
Tinge his brow with sunset glow.
Why should good words ne'er be said
Of a friend till he is dead!

VERSE 6

Greetings are sent to Mary, who the apostle reminds them — 'bestowed much labour for you' (N.Tr.).

VERSE 7

The claims of kindred are not forgotten; but the higher claim to remembrance in the case of Andronicus and Junias is that they had suffered with the apostle as 'fellow prisoners'. The apostle carries out his own exhortation, 'In honour preferring one another' (12:10), for he says they 'are of note among the apostles' and 'were in Christ' before himself.

VERSES 8-9

Amplias and Stachys are saluted not only as beloved but as 'my beloved'. Urban is mentioned as a fellow workman in Christ (N.Tr.).

VERSES 10-11

Appelles, possibly, had passed through specially testing experiences and therefore it may be, is described as 'approved in Christ'. Those who belonged to Aristobulus and Narcissus are saluted but in the case of the latter, the words are added 'which are in the Lord', suggesting that not all his family were the Lord's. Herodion is mentioned as another of his kinsmen.

VERSE 12

Two sisters are saluted who 'labour in the Lord' and one 'which laboured much in the Lord'; seemingly her labours were in the past.

VERSE 13

From Mark 15:21 we may conclude that the father of Rufus had borne the cross of Christ on the way to Golgotha — a service that had its reward, for the son is 'chosen in the Lord'. His mother too is remembered for she had on some occasion acted as a mother to the apostle.

VERSES 14-15

Several brethren are simply mentioned by name, to whom salutations are sent as also to the brethren with them. This may indicate that there were several companies of saints meeting in different parts of the city.

VERSE 16

All are exhorted to manifest their love to one another by saluting 'with an holy kiss'. The ordinary customs of the country in manifesting affection can be used, but in the case of Christians it is to be unfeigned and 'holy'.

VERSES 17-18

The apostle has expressed his delight in all that is beautiful in the saints but, before closing, he utters a word of warning as to those in their midst who were a cause of sorrow. There were even in those early times, some who instead of binding the saints together in love and building them up in the truth, were a cause of division and an occasion of stumbling. The test by which to try and expose such is 'the doctrine which ye have learned'. Both the teaching and practice of such is contrary to sound doctrine. Whatever their pretensions, such serve not the

Lord Jesus Christ. They serve, says the apostle, 'their own belly'; a designedly gross figure to pour contempt upon their personal self importance. Filled with themselves, they were not subject to the Lord. They may indeed assert themselves with good words and fair speeches, for the self important man in seeking to stand well with others, is ever a flatterer. Fair speeches may tend to deceive the hearts of the unsuspecting, but faithfulness to the Lord and love to His people, will lead us to 'avoid' these men. How often experience shows that such are proof against argument and remonstrance and therefore all that can be done is to avoid them. It is no true love to sanction by practical fellowship, those whose self importance, independency of their brethren and insubjection to the Lord, cause division amongst the people of God.

Nothing will more effectually preserve from the harm that such can work, than by carrying out the simple injunction to 'avoid' them. Many might be quite unable to meet such with argument or doctrine, but all, even the simplest, can 'avoid' them. The troubler that is faithfully avoided by the Lord's people, could not long remain with them.

VERSE 19

In contrast to those who 'serve not our Lord Jesus Christ', the apostle can bear witness of the saints at Rome, that their 'obedience is come abroad to all men'. If there were insubject individuals, the body of the Lord's people still walked in subjection to one another and in obedience to the Lord. For this the apostle could rejoice, but for their guidance in regard to evil he says, 'I would have you wise unto that which is good and simple concerning evil'. One has truly said, that 'human wisdom seeks to guard itself by a thorough knowledge of the world and of all evil ways'. The wisdom that comes from above does not need to cul-

THE EPISTLE TO THE ROMANS

tivate acquaintance with evil in order to escape it. '*By the word of Thy lips* I have kept me from the paths of the destroyer' (Psalm 17:10). It is only by the knowledge of the truth that we escape evil. The sheep follow the Shepherd '*for they know His voice*; and a stranger will they not follow ... for they *know not* the voice of strangers' (John 10:4-5). They escape the stranger not because they know his evil teaching, but because 'they know not'. If we know God's path for His people we need not turn aside to acquaint ourselves with the evil of every bye-path of the destroyer. How many have lost their way in seeking to investigate some bye-path which they know to be evil.

Verse 20

To be occupied with evil only plunges the soul into endless controversy and unrest. To walk in simple obedience will be a path of peace and to find that, very soon, all the evil will be dealt with when the God of peace will bruise Satan under our feet. Until then the apostle commits the saints to the all sustaining 'grace of our Lord Jesus Christ'.

Verse 21

The apostle not only sends his personal salutations but, in the fellowship of love, he delights to pass on the salutations of his fellow workers.

Verses 22-24

Love too gives his amanuensis an opportunity to salute the brethren. Gaius, whose hospitality was extended to the apostle, sends greetings. The whole church at Corinth saluted the saints at Rome. Erastus, who held a high civic position sent salutations, and Quartus, a brother.

Again the apostle expresses his desires by repeating the benediction 'The grace of our Lord Jesus Christ be with you all'.

Verses 25-27

Finally, the epistle is closed with an ascription of glory to God. At the beginning of the epistle the apostle tells us that he writes to establish the saints in their relationships with God (1:11). Now, at the close he owns that the power to establish the saints is not in his epistle, but in the God who alone can apply the truths of the gospel to the soul. So he takes no glory to himself as the writer of the epistle, but ascribes all glory to 'Him that is able to *stablish*' according to his gospel.

Further, God can lead us into the deeper truths of Christianity for which the gospel is the necessary foundation. Therefore, he not only says according to my gospel, but also, 'the preaching of Jesus Christ, according to the revelation of the mystery, which was kept secret since the world began'.

These heavenly privileges of the saints, as forming part of the body of Christ, are just alluded to in order to give point to his exhortations (12:4-5) but are not opened up in the epistle. For the unfolding of the mystery of Christ we must pass to the epistle to the Ephesians. Kept secret since the world began this mystery is now revealed through the prophets of New Testament days. This presentation of Christ which makes known the mystery goes out to all nations for the obedience of faith. To the only wise God, Who can give effect to this preaching, be glory through Jesus Christ for ever. Amen.

OTHER BOOKS BY HAMILTON SMITH
FROM SCRIPTURE TRUTH PUBLICATIONS

"THE LORD IS MY SHEPHERD" AND OTHER PAPERS

ISBN 978-0-901860-06-4; (paperback)

97 pages; July 1987

THE GOSPEL OF MARK: AN EXPOSITORY OUTLINE

ISBN 978-0-901860-69-9; (paperback)

ISBN 978-0-901860-70-5; (hardback)

144 pages; March 2007

ELIJAH: A PROPHET OF THE LORD

ISBN 978-0-901860-68-2; (paperback)

80 pages; March 2007

ELISHA: THE MAN OF GOD

ISBN 978-0-901860-79-8; (paperback)

92 pages; March 2007

SHORT PAPERS ON THE CHURCH

ISBN 978-0-901860-80-4; (paperback)

96 pages; March 2008

EXTRACTS FROM THE LETTERS OF SAMUEL RUTHERFORD

ISBN 978-0-901860-81-1; (paperback)

96 pages; March 2008

OTHER BOOKS FROM SCRIPTURE TRUTH PUBLICATIONS
NEW TESTAMENT COMMENTARY SERIES BY F. B. HOLE:

THE GOSPELS AND ACTS

ISBN 978-0-901860-42-2 (paperback)

ISBN 978-0-901860-46-0 (hardback)

392 pages; February 2007

ROMANS AND CORINTHIANS

ISBN 978-0-901860-43-9 (paperback)

ISBN 978-0-901860-47-7 (hardback)

176 pages; February 2007

GALATIANS TO PHILEMON

ISBN 978-0-901860-44-6 (paperback)

ISBN 978-0-901860-48-4 (hardback)

204 pages; February 2007

HEBREWS TO REVELATION

ISBN 978-0-901860-45-3 (paperback)

ISBN 978-0-901860-49-1 (hardback)

304 pages; February 2007

UNDERSTANDING CHRISTIANITY SERIES:

SEEK YE FIRST BY JOHN S BLACKBURN

ISBN 978-0-901860-61-3 (paperback)

ISBN 978-0-901860-02-6 (hardback)

136 pages; February 2007

GOD AND RELATIONSHIPS BY COR BRUINS

ISBN 978-0-901860-36-1 (paperback)

108 pages; August 2006

"THE EPISTLE OF CHRIST" EDITED BY F. B. HOLE
  ISBN 978-0-901860-73-6 (paperback)
  140 pages; March 2008

GOD'S INSPIRATION OF THE SCRIPTURES BY WILLIAM KELLY
  ISBN 978-0-901860-51-4 (paperback)
  ISBN 978-0-901860-56-9 (hardback)
  484 pages; March 2007

LECTURES ON THE CHURCH OF GOD BY WILLIAM KELLY
  ISBN 978-0-901860-50-7 (paperback)
  244 pages; February 2007

  ISBN 978-0-901860-55-2 (hardback)
  244 pages; March 2007

UNDERSTANDING THE OLD TESTAMENT SERIES:

THE GOSPEL IN JOB BY YANNICK FORD
  ISBN 978-0-901860-76-7 (paperback)
  ISBN 978-0-901860-77-4 (hardback)
  112 pages; March 2007

DELIVERING GRACE BY JOHN T MAWSON
  ISBN 978-0-901860-64-4 (paperback)
  ISBN 978-0-901860-78-1 (hardback)
  192 pages; March 2007

LESSONS FROM EZRA BY TED MURRAY
  ISBN 978-0-901860-75-0 (paperback)
  84 pages; March 2007

UNDESTANDING THE NEW TESTAMENT SERIES:

PATMOS SPEAKS TODAY BY JOHN WESTON
  ISBN 978-0-901860-66-8 (paperback)
  88 pages; February 2007

Printed in the United Kingdom
by Lightning Source UK Ltd.
130660UK00001B/175-222/P

9 780901 860859